Springs
in the Desert

from the pens of
Utah Christian Writers Fellowship

Volume 1

Springs in the Desert
from the pens of Utah Christian Writers Fellowship
Volume 1

© 2012 by Utah Christian Writers Fellowship

Published by Next Step Books, P.O. Box 70271, West Valley City, Utah 84170

ISBN-13: 978-1937671037
ISBN-10: 1937671038

Contents

Alphabetical Category Index

Devotional

Fiction

Nonfiction

Poetry and Prayer

Up A Tree

Marcia Hornok

What has trembling legs, pine sap in her hair, and a new outlook on life? A pastor's wife whose husband loves the outdoors (almost) as much as he loves her.

In mid-summer's heat, my husband Ken decides we should take Tuesday off and head into the Utah canyons with our ATV. *Wonderful! A romantic get-away in nature's beauty with my sweetheart.*

So on Tuesday morning, he wakes me at 6 AM. "I thought this was our day off," I protest.

"It is, and we don't want to miss any of it."

I pack our lunch, ice water, tissues, sun block, matches, dry socks—I'm the comfort station on outdoor excursions. Ken hitches up the ATV to the van, and we drive out of town. I snooze until jolted awake on the gravel road that leads to the ATV trails.

Fifteen bumpy miles later, Ken parks the van and says, "Let's leave the ATV here and take a little hike first." Off we go. As the terrain inclines, we adopt our usual hiking pattern: Ken bounds up the hill like a young buck. He stops every 100 yards to wait for me, while I trudge along like a porcupine. I reach him and he takes off again.

After an exhausting hour of this, I begin to wonder how he talked me into this. Do I really want to spend my day off gasping for breath with my sweetheart? I mean sweetheart.

Every time I catch up to him, I voice a mild complaint, but we bound and trudge on. Finally I decide that if he wants to ruin my day, I might as well ruin his. At the next rendezvous, I stage a sit-in. "Why are we doing all this hiking when we brought the ATV? Do we have a goal here other than putting one foot in front of the other? Why did we leave the lunch in the van—I'm hungry." With dramatic flourish, I add, "I think I'm getting altitude sickness."

Then he admits he has a purpose in mind. "I found a tree stand here one day, and I wanted you to see it. It's around here somewhere."

"Haven't we passed ten already?"

"Come on. We've got to be close."

Trudge. Trudge.

A little farther up, he starts looking around. "I know it's in this area."

Trudge. Trudge.

"Just a little more."

Trudge. Trudge.

"Ah! There it is!" He stops and points to a stand of pines 100 feet tall. A crude ladder scales one side. Made of branches and twine, the ladder is a Peter Pan original.

Ken starts climbing with a cheerful, "Follow me!"

I look up into branches so dense, I cannot see the top of the ladder. The rungs, spaced about 18 inches apart, require all my concentration. One hand, the other hand, one foot, the other foot...

Ken keeps asking if I'm all right. I keep wondering how dangerous it will be to get down, assuming I make it up.

Finally the ladder ends—not in a tree stand, but at a large horizontal branch. "Now what?" I holler up to him.

"Walk about six feet out on that branch," he calls down.

I do so and find another medieval ladder. Can't see the top of this one either, and Ken is out of sight, but hopefully still close enough to hear me scream when I fall.

I start up this second ladder. Pinesap sticks to my jeans, my ponytail, and hairs on my arms. That pesky verse in Ephesians comes to mind, "Submit to your husband as to the Lord." *After all, Ken loves me and wants me to be happy.*

Suddenly I flash back to my fortieth birthday when Ken thought up another adventure for us—this one involving skiis and frostbite, but another romantic setting. We got to the resort, and Ken helped me onto the first lift we saw. At the top, we discovered that every trail down was a Black Diamond for expert-only skiers. I burst into tears. It took him over an hour to coax me down that mountain. *Is this another one of those supposed mountain-top experiences? How can I trust him when he does things like that?*

His voice brings me back to the clear and present danger. "Be careful the rungs don't snap. This ladder is pretty old—keep your feet to the outside edges."

Now my thoughts are anything but submissive. *How could he do this to me? What if I fall and break my back 100 miles from civilization?* I think about how sorry he will be when the life-flight helicopter carries me off. *If he loved me he wouldn't treat me like this. I don't deserve it. What other husband makes his 55-year-old wife climb a tree? And he's a pastor! Surely he knows I'm not strong enough.*

Ken is still asking if I'm okay, but I'm crying too hard to answer. I feel stranded—too far up to go back, and no place to stop and rest. I keep climbing with one hand, the other hand, one foot, the other foot. Now my self-talk has changed to Esther 4:16, "If I perish, I perish."

Finally, after 48 rungs (I counted them on the way down), I come eye-level to a platform. It looks like a crude raft with branches lashed together. Ken pulls me through the opening, and there we are—70 feet from the ground, afloat in a treetop.

Gazing to where blue sky meets the limitless horizon, we thrill at the eagle's view of mountains, valleys, and distant lakes. A cool breeze blows on our faces, drying my tears. What scenery. What serenity. I forget how scared I had been as we lean together, mesmerized by the grandeur.

Hugging Ken I say, "Thank you for bringing me here."

That afternoon, while riding behind Ken on the ATV, my arms around his waist, I think about how my morning adventure often parallels my walk with the Lord.

Many times I don't like where He's taking me—it's not what I expected. It seems to have no purpose to it, and there's no end in sight, but it's out of my control. I grumble and keep trudging. I know I should trust God, but I'm scared. And mad at Him—a clear sign of "attitude sickness."

Then when I want to give up, it gets harder! I'm forced into a new situation. *Why doesn't God do something? If He really loves me, why is this happening? What did I do to deserve it? He knows I can't take any more. How can I get out of this mess?* But there I am up a tree of life, stranded on God's sovereignty, with nothing to do but climb.

My independent nature wants to plan my own expeditions. I pray for God to meet my expectations, because after all, they would glorify Him (my way). Instead of a gleeful ride, however, He gives me mountains to climb.

Like when I got a rare cancer at the age of 37 but was mis-diagnosed for the next 14 years while it slowly grew inside my head. I thought I had surrendered everything to God before learning I had cancer, but I still tried to "trust in the Lord with all my intellect." After three surgeries to remove most of my ear along with my hearing on that side, I found God was excising the cancer of self-will from my heart as well.

I had to stop resisting and whisper through tears, "Not my will, but Thine be done." Even if it meant dying young. Not knowing how my children would turn out. No grandbabies. Ken remarrying someone cuter and more submissive than I. She will even love to hike and ski.

Eventually I came to an open place, and God pulled me through. Cancer taught me to accept God's inscrutability. He doesn't need me to figure Him out—just love Him. One of God's 70 questions to Job was, *"Will the one who contends with the Almighty correct Him? Let him who accuses God answer Him!" Then Job answered the Lord: "I am unworthy—how can I reply to You? I put my hand over my mouth"* (Job 40:2-4).

When God gives an unexpected climb, we get a higher view—new vistas of His faithfulness and wisdom. Every trial becomes a venture in trust and an opportunity to exchange our self reliance for His sufficiency. I would rather not have had cancer and hearing loss, but I can agree with Psalm 119:71, "It was good for me to be afflicted so that I might learn Your decrees."

Thank You, Lord, for bringing me here.

The next time I'm up a tree, I'll try to remember to submit without a struggle. Losses teach lessons I cannot learn any other way, and griefs can bring gifts in disguise.

When I surrender to God in my hardships, it builds my spiritual muscles. Then my relationship with Him becomes an exciting romantic adventure.

This article originally appeared in *Discipleship Journal*, January-February, 2007.

Moses and Me

Josiah Marshall

An image stares at me, hanging from the wall, with murder in his eyes...

Silence taunts Moses as his desperate yells fall flat as he sinks into a hole of desert. The stillness, emptiness of despair mutes his cry, convincing him God has given up. Mirages play out his past, burning inadequacies, insecurity and inferiority into memory; fueling beasts of fear and loneliness that ravage his soul and constrict his chest. Parched and dry shimmers of heated glass reflect the grisly, contorted features of these beasts on his worn, haggard face. Imprisoned by life's vindictive Hater darkness isolates him from all he once knew. Embittered Moses lies huddled under cold starless nights trying to ignore the searing touch of FAILURE.

Succumbing to loss and misery a spark is born. Piercing his darkness color bathes his eyes in a constant dance of fire. Instead of Death he is drawn by a glow of unflickering, undying life. Washed in its light he is licked ablaze with anticipation. Refreshed in its cool embrace his face shines anew. Submerged in a love so sweet he is cleansed of all fear and doubt. Relief and peace swell his heart as its heat transforms the past, refining his experience. Called, destined to live free he stumbles from deaths rubble sobbing in the dazzling warm arms of HOPE.

Fragrance of life fills him as an oasis of love and acceptance. His eyes flare as dormant promises reawaken; truth and meaning course through his veins. Tickled by the soft touch of a joyous breeze the Fathers whisper assures. Never forsaken, never forgotten his heart swells with excitement and he trusts the pull of His voice. Seeding His word deep within him his feet stand firm, vision focused. Step by step Moses is filled with the joy of confidence, certainty and faith as his past strengthens the Father's mantle of PURPOSE.

The image I see is myself with the past intent of self-murder.

Fig-uratively Speaking

Kim Malkogainnis

Members of one congregation were socializing after the morning service, and conversation turned to the sermon. The pastor had spoken about Jesus' encounter with an unfruitful fig tree.

People made various comments before one woman piped up, "Well, this morning's message has inspired me to take action."

"What do you plan to do?" someone asked.

"I'm going straight to the store to buy cookies," she replied, with a wink. "I have a sudden craving for a fig newton."

Kimberly Malkogainnis, Copperton, Utah. Christian Reader, "Lite Fare."

The Narrow Trail

Virginia Smith

"Because strait is the gate and narrow is the way, which leadeth unto life, and few there be that find it." (Matthew 7:14)

In Utah's Wasatch Mountains just east of Salt Lake City there's a trail I love to hike. It's called Donut Falls. I drive up Big Cottonwood Canyon and leave my car at a small and often crowded parking area, lace up my hiking boots and take off. There are two trails—the first is wide enough for a car, though no vehicles are permitted up there. It is easy, with a gentle grade and few rocks littering the way. It's a beautiful hike and leads to the top of the falls where I can see the donut, a giant flat rock with a round hole where thousands of gallons of rushing mountain water pour through.

The second trail isn't so easy. It's narrow, steep and often jagged. I stop periodically to catch my breath, and at one place I have to climb down a six-foot muddy ledge, holding on to tree roots for balance. But it's worth the extra effort, because the narrow trail ends below the falls instead of above it. All that water pours through the hole above me and thunders into a sheltered pool, refreshing me with a cool mountain spray as it rushes past me over a stunning rocky creek bed. The view from that angle takes my breath away. It's well worth the struggle to get there.

Jesus spoke of a difficult road we must take, one that leads to life. It is not as easy as the wide road, but I like to think it's like the narrow trail to Donut Falls. What waits for us at the end is well worth the effort.

This devotional first appeared online in 2010 at ChristianDevotions.US

Stained

Mark Francis

Fearing what I was about to face, I pull my knees close and bury my head. The cold floor and wall of the crowded cell intensify the growing anguish that convulses my body. Still reeling from a myriad of thoughts, the truth plays over and over in my mind that I deserve what is coming. Without looking up, I can hear the sounds of others wrestling with the same apprehension. Crying and anger mix to create an atmosphere of panic that terrorizes each convict. Some accept their fate with profound resignation, while others continue to deny the truth with stubborn bitterness.

All at once the room falls silent. Approaching footsteps announce that which we fear. Ignoring the pain from sitting on the cement floor, I press harder against the back wall, hoping to go unnoticed. Still, the fear drives me to know what's happening. I slowly stand to my feet, my heart failing with the scene before me. Each prisoner, silenced by the unalterable reality of their guilt, reservedly moves to line up in single fashion for the march to "The Chamber of Justice." Wild imaginations flood my mind as the grip of death takes hold of my broken heart. Knowing I have no choice, I join the line, coldness sweeping over me with haunting vengeance.

We walk for what seems like hours, our appointment with death growing with sinister power. Even the passageway from our cell to the chamber echoes with the growing prelude of our demise. Memories flood my mind like never before, but end with the same pronouncement seemingly loud enough for others to hear..." You've failed. Hope is gone." Pure fear poisons my heart, as all I can do is keep moving. Lost in my private pit of despair, I don't notice the door approaching marking our arrival.

The massive chamber looms large. Rows and rows of fellow prisoners stand side by side in circular fashion around an upright wooden post located towards the center of the chamber. Hushed silence marks the growing sea of condemned humanity, each inmate experiencing the sickening awe of the moment. Several guards, each strong and perceivably vile, stand at attention around the single center post, their laughing eyes filled with what seems like drunken ecstasy. Trembling, I cry to die before the anticipated violence is unleashed.

Taking my place and standing in the first row of my section, I notice movement from off to my left. Prisoners part as another set of guards escort a lone man to just in front of the central post. Maliciously stripping off his clothes, the guards then tie his wrists to the large ring attached to the top of the post. Standing silently with both arms stretched upward, the man raises his head and slowly scans the crowded chamber before him. Desperately wanting some kind of comfort, I determine to hold my gaze if his eyes come to mine. My heart races as we connect. What I see sends a shiver through my body. Deep and penetrating, resoluteness fills his stare, along with a small, but obvious smile. Perplexed and overwhelmed, I look away, my stomach churning.

What crazy person is this? I wonder, painful silence flooding my soul.

Suddenly, my thoughts are interrupted as a terrorizing strong hand grabs my left arm and barks, "This way!"

Jolted, I barely can walk, realizing the reality of the moment. We move towards the center area and stop a few feet behind the tied prisoner. A separate guard bends down and unlocks one of dozens of wooden trunks stacked just to the side of the center post. Too dazed to notice, I am unaware he retrieves something from the trunk. Quickly he comes to where I'm standing, takes my hands and places something in them. Looking down, I'm horrified. A large leather whip with numerous tails rests in my hands. Attached down each tail are pieces of sharpened hard objects, each one inscribed. Almost as by design, the writings enlarge and begin to glow, capturing my attention. As I cannot but help to read the inscriptions, my heart sinks deeper into a dark pit of guilty shame. Each inscription names a specific place, time and accounting of my history where my arrogant pride and selfishness led my heart. After reading only a few, I look away letting go of the whip. Guilt increases its weight upon me as I fall to the ground, vomiting what little I had left in my twisted stomach.

Angrily, the guard jerks me back to my feet. I can barely breathe waiting for the noose to close around my hands and be led to the post for my punishment. Instead, I'm pushed just a short distance away from the tied prisoner. Laughingly and with mocking eyes, the guard again places the whip into my hands. Drawing close to my face where his stench fills the air, he coldly says, "Use it."

It takes a moment before the realization hits me. I stare at the whip, then at the bare backside of this fellow prisoner in front of me. My mind jumbles as I don't understand. I start to turn to question when a crashing blow lands squarely on the side of my face.

"USE IT!" comes the demand again, this time filled with deep hatred.

Turning back to face the tied fellow prisoner, I slowly raise the studded whip. My first blow lands short as I convulse again with horrifying shame.

Another blow strikes the base of my back from behind as the guard shouts, "HIT HIM!"

Slowly, I again lift the whip and with sickening force send it to the prisoner's back. Each tail sinks deep into his flesh sending a tremor throughout his body. I hold the whip still, not wanting to cause more pain. A strong hand grabs my own and violently pulls back, ripping open the flesh and sending blood in all directions. The gruesome sight hits me deeply, again weakening my legs under me.

"Keep going," the command comes. Barely sane, I continue.

I lose track of time before a shrill "Enough!" echoes in my ear. Finally able to stop, I look down and realize I'm stained red from head to toe. My self-made whip, now crimson, drips with another man's bloodied flesh. Ashamed and tormented, I cannot look upon my victim. *What have I done?*

Fear rises quickly as I expect that my turn has come in this sick and twisted punishment. Ready to be ordered to the post, a guard instead strips the whip from my hand and roughly pushes me towards a nearby row of prisoners. Several step aside to let me pass as a door opens behind them. As I stumble through the opening, I can barely see, sweat and blood mixing in my eyes. The guard stops and jerks me back around, putting his face only inches from mine. Speaking with calculated but controlled bitterness, his words confound me.

"You're free. Your punishment has been served." With that, he turns and re-enters the chamber, closing the door behind him.

Overwhelmed and broken, I fall to the ground unable to process what just happened. My thoughts jumbled, I can do nothing but weep violently. Time slows when finally one

word rises in my heart as I replay the horrid experience...
Why?

Quiet, but intimately powerful, I hear the answer penetrate my heart as I try and rub away the red stain upon my skin...

"Deeply loved and desired, what you could not do has been done for you. You are forever stained with freedom's blood."

City Park

Angela Rednour

The sounds of nature
Amongst the bustle of life
Calm lakes shimmer
Giant trees give shade
Beautiful flowers bloom; then fade

A park in the city
What a wonderful thing
Peace in the midst
Of chaos and steam

A place for the runners
Joggers and thinkers
A place for the children
The dogs and the readers

A place where one goes
To see nature and beauty
To get away from the world
Of hustle and hurry.

Grand Escape

Rose Turnbow

They prevented me in the day of my calamity: but the LORD was my stay. He brought me forth also into a large place: he delivered me, because he delighted in me. (1 Samuel 22:19-20)

"Mr. Larsen is out back and he caught a mouse" I yelled to Mom, as I ran in from our backyard.

Mr. Larsen owned the neighborhood grocery store next to our house. The garbage bins behind the store contained old wilted vegetables, meat scraps, and other smelly things which attracted mice.

Our four cats usually kept the mice at bay, but we still occasionally found one in our home. My brother and I would laugh at Mom as she ran around the kitchen, chasing the mouse with a broom. Mom was relentless in her quest to rid our home of the furry little creatures.

One snowy morning we were enjoying breakfast when my sister squealed and pointed to a wiggling box of cookies on the counter. Dad jumped up, grabbed the box and peeked inside. A mouse peered back at him.

"Get it out of here!" yelled Mom, as she jumped up and went for the broom. Dad held the top of the box closed as he hurried to get the mouse outside. Dashing out the front door, Dad called "Kitty, Kitty! Here, Kitty, Kitty!" Our four cats came running and gathered around Dad's legs, mewing excitedly, begging for the treasure he had for them.

Dad opened the box and dumped the contents right in the center of the circle of cats. The mouse flopped out in the snow and crouched among the cookies and cats.

All four cats leaped at the pile of cookies. The mouse scurried under the cats' legs and darted toward the street. Munching on the cookies, the cats completely ignored the mouse.

"There it is! Get the mouse! There it goes!" Dad yelled. He pointed at the mouse as it scurried down the driveway, leaving little foot prints in the newly fallen snow. Dad ran to the sidewalk and watched the mouse disappear.

The cats were eating their treats as Dad stomped back in the house. "Some mousers!" he grumbled—then laughed—as he shook the snow off of his boots.

The mouse, in a dire situation, was delivered from the jaws of the cats by a few cookies. Like the mouse, who was destined to be destroyed, we are rescued and taken care of by our loving Father. He removes us from calamity because He delights in us, His children.

Staying on the Vine

Mary Jo Sanger

How does the branch bear fruit? Not from air, sunshine nor water alone, it must leaf out, blossom and abide on the vine. (John 15:1-12.)

Pruning may be needed, the process painful at the time, but, as we abide in Christ the end results bear plentiful, sweet fruit. (John 15: 2b.) "Every branch that bears fruit HE prunes that it may bear more fruit."

When the gentle loving hand of the Lord has pared us of unsightly habits: anger, bitterness, unbelief or fear, we look to the Lamb of God who is able – yea- more than able to keep that which we have committed to Him. (Jude 24.)

Abiding moment by moment in Christ as His word abides in us; we have joy unspeakable, walk in peace and are filled with His glory. I received joy when I finally understood that abiding in Christ is a vocation—not a location.

Each and every day Satan as the deceiver comes to tempt us, as we're renewed in Christ daily we recognize Satans' tactics, turn away from him and dwell in peace. (Colossians 3:16-17.)

2 Corinthians 4:8-9, 16-18

We are troubled on every side, yet not distressed; we are perplexed, but not in despair; Persecuted, but not forsaken; cast down, but not destroyed;

For our light affliction, which is but for a moment, worketh for us a far more exceeding and eternal weight of glory; While we look not at the things which are seen, but at the things which are not seen: for the things which are seen are temporal; but the things which are not seen are eternal.

How shall a CHRISTIAN bear fruit?

Every new believer has trials and obstacles to overcome; Song of Solomon 2:15 admonishes us to catch the "little" foxes. The little foxes spoil the vines.

It's the little things that trip us up and discourage us in our walk with the Lord, as we read and study God's word He admonishes us to be of good cheer, and be strong in the Lord and the power of His might, Ephesians 6: 10-19.

Galations 2:20

I am crucified with Christ: nevertheless I live; yet not I, but Christ liveth in me: and the life which I now live in the flesh I live by the faith of the Son of God, who loved me, and gave himself for me.

Remember: Hebrews 13:5

Greater Thoughts
Mark Francis

"How precious also are thy thoughts unto me, O God! How great is the sum of them!" (Psalm 139:17)

"Stop thinking that!" I told myself over and over. Taunting images and harassing voices filled my mind. Trying hard to shift my focus, the tempting thoughts returned, more powerful than before. It seemed the harder I worked to rid myself of this mental poison, the more it filled my mind. Feeling condemned and weak, I wondered if victory was even possible.

Many of us believe we cannot conquer our thought lives. Daily struggles and apparent failures over relationships and personal behaviors, added to the general temptations of life can multiply discouragement in our heart. Before long we find ourselves drawn to numbing habits or addictions hoping to lessen the pain.

While we strive to quit thinking, God encourages us to think more. His answer to a pure thought life lies in dwelling more upon what God says about our lives than trying harder to keep impure things out.

Like unlimited grains of sand on a long beach, the sheer number of God's enduring thoughts about our lives overwhelms our best imaginations. Hope, encouragement, vision, joy and wisdom fill His heart for us, and He desires to constantly share these personal, solid truths each day.

As we quiet ourselves to hear His heart, a growing integrity will mark our inner experiences. The supremacy and power of His thoughts crush all other judgments, as God declares the timeless truth of our lives. Dwelling upon His opinions creates the inner purity we seek.

Grace Personified

Irene Champlin

It was Christmas Eve. *Grace* came all done up in a black carrying case, tired from her journey from New York City to Las Vegas. She came with her mistress. No, *she* was the mistress, and soon was going to make all of us very much aware of that.

The household *Grace* entered that late night consisted of a Grandma, her son and his wife and two grandchildren so there was a three-generational spread. The family hadn't seen Grandma for a number of years so *Grace* came to bridge the gap. She was a silly, white-wiggly thing.

Grandma first became aware of her presence as she ran out from nowhere right under her feet as she was making coffee the next morning. That's how *Grace* comes so often, on silent, padded feet, begging for attention. We are frequently just too busy to see her there.

Grace doesn't play favorites. She is willing to be with, or go with anyone who will show her some attention. *Grace* is like that!

The rattle of the dog harness by anyone in the family who held it got immediate response. Like a streak of white lightning she would run to it and even put her head right in it, begging to go for a walk.

Sometimes *Grace* interfered with the direction we wanted to go. She balked, almost audibly saying, "Not *that* way!" At other times she wanted to talk with everyone on the way, and we were too busy to care. We are not very *graceful.*

Brother Matthew liked *Grace,* at a distance. If she got too close to his bare toes she soon found out that she wasn't his favorite! But buffeted or not, *Grace* went slithering back.

A tired, and somewhat smelly Matthew, fresh (or unfresh) from the gym, stretched out full length on the sofa, bare arms behind his head. Never mind that *Grace* had been buffeted, or that Matthew was rather "odoriferous." She curled up beside him, her head in his armpit and the two of them slept! *Grace* is like that! "Did you hurt me? Of course you did, but just accept me into your life and I'll forgive you," is what *Grace* says.

When all is happy and peaceful in the family *Grace* is there to bless. Her antics at trying to be part of the fun go to great *heights.* She became "super-dog" at the Christmas gathering as she jumped higher than she was tall to try to get a tasty morsel off the table. Oh that we'd always let *Grace* entertain us!

Sometimes we forget her and for a while she goes off and does her own thing. Yes, we sort of see her running around, but ignore her. We're like that with *Grace!* She comes back once more, however, and makes her presence felt. She lies on the back of the sofa as we read a book, still ignoring her and puts her head lovingly on our shoulder. *Grace* is pleading to not be ignored. *She* is like that! Although sister Sarah isn't there *Grace* takes comfort in her coat which she has left on the sofa—she sniffs it, rolls it into a ball and makes her bed out of it.

Then it is time for the generations of the family to again go their separate ways. Does *Grace* go with them until they are once more joined? *She* would like to do that.

I bet you are thinking that Grace is a little dog. She is. But *Grace* is also a metaphor meaning HOW WE TREAT EACH OTHER.

Henry James, who was a famous author, was asked by his nephew, "What should I do with my life?" James replied, "There are three things you should do. (His nephew, with his brow furrowed, was waiting to hear something like the labors of Hercules). The three great labors that he was talking about were: "Be gentle! Be gentle! Be gentle!"

Instead

Marcia Hornok

Forgive my inflated view of self.
What I deserve instead
      Are painful torture, cruel abuse,
      And thorns pressed in my head.

I deserve to die for my sins;
Instead You were falsely blamed,
      For crimes You were not guilty of,
      Arrested—sentenced—shamed.

Instead of getting what I deserve,
You gave me what I need:
      Mercy in exchange for my sin,
      Your name, Your home, Your creed,

A way of living that's free from self,
      Supply for every loss,
      Joy and peace, unlimited love—

Because You took my cross.

Sharing Our Burdens

Mark Francis

"Bear ye one another's burdens, and so fulfil the law of Christ." (Galatians 6:2)

Weeks had passed and still relief eluded my heart. Months before, a co-worker had spread degrading lies about a personal relationship. On the surface, the lies seemed to be accepted as true, even though the character of my life proved otherwise. Daily I swung from being undeniably angry to deeply hurt, but I struggled forward. I questioned God continually, asking "Where is my justice?"

During an especially trying week, I met a close friend for breakfast. For some time, we had been meeting weekly to share our experiences and pray together. Until this point, I had chosen to keep my distressed circumstances to myself not wanting to burden him. But that day was different. Feeling weak and vulnerable, I decided to reveal my trial and ask for prayer.

With deep love, his words to God opened my heart. Slowly I began to weep as my burden lifted and fresh hope brought renewed strength. His insight and encouragement helped to steady my despairing heart and restore vision of God's faithful compassion. The healing I needed had begun.

God created us for companionship, whether celebrating great success or bringing encouragement to one's troubled heart. Just as Jesus continually reminded his friends of God's close help in difficult times, we can offer the same as we receive the Holy Spirit's direction in our prayers for others. Burdens become lighter when held by many hands.

Awakening

Angela Rednour

There is nothing in the distance but never ending gray water. It's early and I'm the only one awake. My knees are pulled to my chin, arms wrapped around them. The sun is rising at my back and the only noise I hear is the gentle whoosh of the calm sea as the water glides up and down the beach.

I sit on the back steps of the rental house. The vastness of the ocean makes me feel an overwhelming sense of peace and I imagine myself on a life raft in the middle of nowhere, with no land in sight.

A small toad hops out of the grass onto the sidewalk in front of the stairs. The soft plopping sound he makes awakens me from the dream-like state I had been lulled into by the sea. Fascinated, I watch as the frog jumps about oblivious to my presence.

I am completely still as I watch him attempt to jump onto the first step. He fails, but tries again and again; he is just too small for such a big step. His failed attempts amuse me. I let out a small giggle. This frightens him and he hops back into the safety of the grass.

By now the sky is alive with pinks, reds and oranges and the world seems to be waking with the ever brightening atmosphere. Birds begin chattering in the tress and in the distance I can see dolphins jumping out of the water.

A pair of binoculars sits near me; I grab them and look at the pod of large sea mammals leaping for joy at the start of a new day. This activity lasts ten minutes before they go about the rest of their daily routine. In the afternoon we will swim out to the area and take photos with our underwater cameras and hope they will want to play with us.

I hear creaking footsteps inside the house and I know I won't be alone much longer. Looking out at the ocean once more, I sigh and try to hold on to the peaceful spell that had bound me just moments before. The sea is still gray in color and still calm, but with the sun glinting off the surface it has an added harshness to it.

There are whispered murmurs inside. A faint odor of coffee has reached me through the open window in the kitchen. The spell is broken. New noises are erupting around me every second. I take a deep breath of the salty air and stretch. My shirt is starting to stick to my back as the sun warms the humid air.

I sigh once more and heave myself into a standing position. As I turn to go into the house I see a gecko scurry across the porch and slither up the wall. I glance back at the ocean once more. The sea now sounds like a hum in the background. I look forward to tomorrow morning when I can be lulled back into the peacefulness of the vast ocean once more.

The Honor Offering

Mark Francis

"Be kindly affectioned one to another with brotherly love; in honour preferring one another." (Romans 12:10)

The resistance of my heart to the simple prompting bothered me. Waiting for the start of the swim meet, a coach of another team settled himself nearby to gain a clearer view of his swimmers. His reputation within our swimming community was not good, and each encounter I had with him brought me to the same conclusion. Aloof and arrogant, he almost always caused problems. Still, I couldn't deny the leading I sensed.

Finally quelling my mixed emotions, I made my decision and approached. He received my handshake with a questioning look.

"Say, I wanted to thank you for all you did putting on the championship meet a few weeks ago. My daughter participated and had a great meet. I know these events take a lot of time and energy. Thanks for doing it."

For a brief moment, he looked puzzled and then a small smile came across his face. Now firmly shaking my hand, his insightful response was not what I expected.

"Wow... a thank you? Normally, all I get are angry people calling me names or worse. I think this is a first. Thanks. You made my day."

Turning to go, my heart was humbled. I once again underestimated the immeasurable worth of affirming others. Reputation or not, his life was worth my meager offering.

Jesus loves acknowledging the true significance of our lives. Desiring that we do the same, the Holy Spirit lives to help us share what God sees of value in others.

These Years
For our 34th Wedding Anniversary

Teresa Hanly

We are learning of Grace unbending
Of mercy poured out on all our wounds
Forgiveness closing the space between us
And of a greater Love that becomes the glue

We are looking to God to help us
The past to learn from and leave behind
Unfettered by the pain sin brings us
Humbled by Love crucified

We are learning to live The Word in action.
Reaping more love to give away
Lord sanctify us for your Glory
And this union be Yours
Our offering

Downscaling Christmas

Kimberley D. Malkogainnis

If you're addicted to a holiday high that ends with you in the dumps, try these ideas.

Start close to home

Get on your knees with your family, and covenant with God to simplify your life. Determine to glorify and worship your external Lord rather than the holiday myth of overworking yourself into exhaustion for a "perfect" Christmas season.

Ask family members which traditions they most want to continue, and ask them to give something in exchange. If your daughter craves homemade cookies, ask her to do the vacuuming or errands to free your time and energy to help her bake. If your family needs a decorated evergreen to make them feel jolly, ask them to take over; explain that your job will be taking snapshots or video of the activity. If they're too young to pitch in, you're fortunate, because you can start them off with simpler traditions.

Question the seemingly immutable. One year, my husband and I and our kids decided not to erect a tree. Instead, we created a small handmade nativity. It was the focus of our celebration that year, and we spent many evenings sipping cider and creating a life-like and heart-expanding scene. Several years later, we donated the project to our church, where it's displayed in the foyer at Christmastime.

Recognize other events throughout the year instead of focusing on "the big one" and all the things it's come to be. Instead of sending Christmas cards, recognize the significance of Easter or Thanksgiving. Mail your family newsletter on your wedding anniversary. Send faxes, emails, or electronic cards anytime just to remind someone that they're loved by you and God.

Instead of making the family portrait a holiday affair, take advantage of summertime reunions, a day at the water slides, a child's school program, or Sunday dinner. Take snapshots and enlarge one.

Reach out

If you're part of a group that usually exchanges gifts, talk to them about alternatives. Agree to exchange only photos, or a service such as babysitting. Suggest adopting a needy group, missionary, family, or charity instead of giving one another yet another thing that doesn't fit, won't last, or (worst of all) needs dusting.

Arrange to have your holiday parties at public places so you (and others in the group) don't have to prepare and clean up. Remember: the goal is simplicity. Fancier eateries mean more complicated, expensive plans and ensembles.

Combine purposes by making your party a gift-wrapping, cookie-baking, or decorating party. Go bowling, miniature golfing, or skating, and enjoy the getting-together instead of the preparation. Go caroling or put in a shift at a soup kitchen; then adjourn to a local coffeehouse for a warm up. Make a special effort to remember and include those who are experiencing their first holiday after losing a loved one.

Give simply

If you choose to give (and it is a choice), make it your goal to give at least one item that expresses Christ's love, whether in word or in deed. Increase your personal quota each year.

Spend the year collecting family recipes. Then distribute copies of the collection—or create a family birthday book or directory. Write a poem or story, or paint a picture especially for your spouse or your mother. Frame a child's finger painting masterpiece or finger prints for a grandparent.

If you normally do fall canning, do a couple of extra jars and set them aside to be used as Christmas gifts. Do the same with summer herbs: Make herbal vinegars or potpourri to give.

Don't be tempted to put something on your charge card and call it a gift. You don't really own anything you buy on time, and you can't give what doesn't belong to you.

Divide your list into paydays and purchase items throughout the year. Each time you shop, try to buy one gift—even a small gift certificate or prepaid phone card. Buy "out of season," for instance, a set of garden tools on summer clearance; slippers, gloves, mittens on winter closeout. Take advantage of fragrance sets that are popular around Mother's Day and Valentine's Day. Pick up extra certificates when you go out to dinner or the movies.

Buy from home-service companies like Avon or Tupperware that deliver to your home. Save time and postage by selecting and purchasing out-of-town gifts at chains that allow the recipient to pick up the gift at a location near them.

Give things to lessen someone else's holiday stress: a book of stamps, wrapping paper, gift bags, tree lights.

If you make gifts, mass-produce them. That is, give everyone a jar of home-canned apple jelly or a special bookmark. That way, you can buy supplies in quantity and focus on doing one thing well.

Pass along something of yours. Give your sister the Barbie doll you used to fight over. Maybe your friend collects thimbles, and you happen to possess a unique one.

Shop odd places: garage sales, antique and junk stores, bazaars. Pick up unusual items if you travel.

Don't wait for Christmas morning to open gifts. We open things that come in the mail whenever they arrive. If someone visits, we exchange and open gifts then. And we usually exchange everything else on Christmas Eve. This helps take our focus off the gift opening, and allows us several small, more meaningful exchanges. It's especially helpful for children who are easily overwhelmed by a flurry of paper and packages.

Make an effort to do kindnesses every day. Contribute regularly to a homeless shelter. Offer to babysit for a single parent. Visit a nursing home resident or shut-in neighbor who has no nearby family or friends. Help carry someone's packages or clean another's windshield of frost if you're physically able. When you see someone who's rushed, let him or her in line in front of you. Take a cup of cocoa to the crossing guard. Smile. Say something outrageous and unexpected like, "God bless you." Be open to opportunities—however brief—to share the gospel message.

The key to downscaling and de-stressing your holidays is having the right attitude. This isn't about the Grinch trying to steal Christmas. It's about a child of the King endeavoring to give others more of God, and give God more of you.

The first Christmas was a gathering of humble people and heavenly hosts whose greatest joy was simply to gaze upon the Savior of mankind. It helps me to remember that I need to clear away the clutter if the world is going to have a chance to see him still.

Springs in the Desert

Originally published in: *Marriage Partnership*, 2009, Web-only

Ice Cream Therapy

Julie Turvey Scott

"Come on. We're going to do some ice cream therapy," I told my son. We'd spent a discouraging day house-hunting in an inflated rental market. With his dad at work, and his sister at camp, just nine-year old Skeeter and I were home. I was ready to take my last $4.00 and indulge. He offered to donate his $2.00. We would go to the ice cream parlor across town and share that huge, expensive, banana split.

Heading out in our gas-guzzling car, second thoughts nagged me. "Skeeter, I wonder if we should spend the rest of our money. It's still two days until payday, and this trip will use most of our gas."

"We could get a soft-serve cone," Skeeter offered brightly.

"No! I don't feel THAT frugal. How about if we go to the grocery store and get some ice cream and a jar of topping? We can enjoy it *several* times, and Dad can have some, too."

"Sure!" he responded with a wiggle.

The splashy orange sign at the store announced a sale: five-quart buckets of ice cream for $2.99. Perfect! We chose vanilla. Skeeter decided to forgo topping because we already had homemade strawberry jam, chocolate syrup and bananas. And who needs whipped cream? He grinned when I handed back his $2.00 as we dashed to the quick check lane.

"That will be $4.99 plus tax," the cashier announced. "That's $5.21 total."

"Oh no," I replied. "This was on sale for $2.99."

She countered, "Well, in that case, you get an *additional* dollar discount, according to store policy."

WOW! Now *I* had $2.00 left, too. We made a beeline for the car.

As we chattered about saving money, banana splits, and this blessing, Skeeter peered into the bag and announced, "Mom, all of the other buckets said 'T.V. brand.' This one doesn't."

Gulp.

The ice cream we chose really *was* $4.99. Here we were, nearly home. Our excitement wilted faster than you could say *melting ice cream*.

And then Skeeter said in a soft voice, "We should go back, huh? It would be the right thing to do."

Indeed.... Like Mary, I treasured in my heart my young son's honesty, even though it would come with a higher price tag.

The cash drawer lay on the counter as the clerk closed her register for the night. I admitted my mistake and apologized. She told us to go get the store-brand ice cream, and still didn't charge us for the difference.

Our second trip home found us praising God even more. Skeeter quoted a line from a kids' radio drama: "Doing right is its own reward." Skeeter *felt* rewarded.

After I prepared the banana splits, Skeeter raised his hand and politely said, "Stop!" He folded his hands, scrunched his eyes tight and prayed, "Thank You, Lord, for helping us do the right thing. Amen."

Banana splits never tasted better.

Seasons of Matrimony

L.T. Kodzo

Some days blow in like winter
Words cut and chafe like blizzard winds
We can't feel each other
Through the gloves we wear

Some days grow soft like spring
Surprising as a blooming bud and
Scrumptious as ripe fruit
Just waiting to be plucked

Some days heat up like summer
Starting too early and ending too late
An exhaustive amount of energy spent
Just looking for shade

Some days just fall into place like autumn
The anticipation of learning fills the air
As kids wander back to school we remember
Everything we forgot about love

Small Blessings

Angela Rednour

Last night as I sat down for a dinner of chicken and dumplings with my cousins the power went out. There was a storm raging outside. Winds so strong they were breaking windows in houses in some areas of the city. Trees were falling over and lightning was a serious threat to anyone foolish enough to be caught outside.

A hush fell over the family and we listened to the storm. It only lasted a second before there was a groan from the electronic loving teenagers of the family, barking from frightened dogs and concern over the house getting too hot without the air conditioner from the adults.

As the storm raged outside, and the family inside, I sat on the couch whispering a prayer that the storm wouldn't create any tornados. I'm deathly afraid of them. I can handle strong wind, power outages and lightning, just keep me away from spinning tunnels of destruction.

Today there wasn't a cloud in the sky. Usually after a storm like this one it creates unbearable heat and humidity in the eastern states, but not today. It was a perfect temperature, with a very soft, cool breeze. In the evening I sat outside with a good book and enjoyed the golden rays of the setting sun. It was my blessing after the storm, both literally and figuratively.

This morning I found out my step-dad passed away. This seems to be the peak in a string of frustrating, unfair circumstances I've had recently. As I sat outside thinking over the past two or three months, going over all the bad in my life I felt the light wind brush over my face and arms. One of those gentle wafts of air that comes directly at you, caressing your skin. I closed my eyes and lifted my head towards the rays of the setting sun. For that one moment, everything was perfect. There was no sadness in my life, no pain. God hugged me with the wind and filled me with peace.

When all of life seems to be going wrong it can be hard to see the blessings in life, but there is always something. It may be small, it may only last a second or two, but it's there, a sunny day, the song of a bird or a warm hug from the wind. These moments are my favorite, especially when they come unexpectedly, at a point when it seems nothing will ever be right again. These small blessings are a relief, a break to give strength to go on, continue the day and conquer the bad moments in life. I think God gives us these small blessings when we are whispering a prayer to God, to keep the tornados away. When we say,

"God, I'm in the worst storm of my life right now, please, please don't let me go through a tornado too."

You may not hear anything right away, the storm may still be raging around you, but soon, very soon, you'll find those few seconds of relief and they will make all the difference in the world. I found those few seconds in a cool breeze and they stayed with me. In my spirit I still feel God hugging me. Even though there is still pain and sadness His peace is, and will continue to give me the comfort I need to make it though.

How does Grandma Drive?

Mary Jo Sanger

Since the "awesome" event of turning 70 will affect me sooner than later, I decided that in the interest of my future venturing out and about—traveling the highways and by-ways, it would benefit me to take a poll. You know, being a Grandma and almost of "the age" it would be advantageous to plan ahead and see what was taking place on the busy motorways.

Watching "Grandma" behind the wheel of her car was entertaining. While on reconnaissance I took particular interest in situations around me and paid attention to her driving skills.

Amazingly, she's courteous. Grandma does not keep the state motto alive – which is: You're first after me!

She does not tailgate. Reading the license plate of the car in front, generously she leaves plenty of room to see the rear tires of the car. She doesn't crowd, just in case the dude who is tail-gaiting behind rams into her rear. There won't be a ticket for hitting the car in front.

There's no blare of the horn—no making it sound like a trumpet or a drum. No brouhaha for her. She is not horn happy. If the car in front is a little slower getting off the starting gate, patience is her middle name; besides, "What's the hurry?" We all stop at the next red light together anyway!

Being meticulous about appearances; Grandma puts on her make-up or jewelry before leaving the house. Hairspray is liberally applied to her satisfaction. A small hurricane would not budge her hair. She takes no chances of it flying in her eyes if the window is open while driving.

Eating or drinking while driving is out! Murphy's Law—the potentate of spills with projectiles is usually alive and well; always spilling on her front. When a spill occurs Grandma is often too far away to run home and change, it's best to heed carefulness and not throw caution to the wind.

Grandma loves to talk on the phone, talking or driving takes her full concentration, experience has taught her to be aware of the dangers of distractions. Her gizmo loving grandson tells her that spending money for one of those new head thingamagiggers is a good investment. She goes shopping, tries one on in the store and looks very carefully – Does it mess up her hair? Purchasing the head thingy allows her both hands on the wheel. Whatever her destination—she can talk.

Grandkids are precious gifts that bring joy to her life. Buckling up her treasures before going into traffic is essential. She's the boss also the keeper of the goodies, so without any back talk or hassles they stay buckled up.

Speeding and weaving in and out of traffic is not something "Grandma" is comfortable with, she likes to mosey along. Whizzing in or out to get ahead of the one car in front is not what makes her day. Impolite to other drivers and being discourteous with hand gestures is just not something she thinks of in a hurry. Grandma was raised to be mannerly.

Last, but not least, she lets other drivers merge into her lane when she can, if she's at a light and someone is off to the side waiting—Grandma lets them in ... With a smile!

Who's dangerous on the roads? It's not always Grandma!

A Living Legacy

Samuel Wilson

The past we contemplate, unable to live it again.
Time keeps moving on; our fight with it is vain.
We cannot repeat our life and change the things we've
done.
The future is too far away for us to look upon.
So live today with thought in mind that it may be our last.
Treat everyone with love and respect—our legacy to pass.

This poem originally appeared in *CHERA Fellowship* magazine, Summer
2011

Symbols and Keys

Virginia Smith

Captain Curtis Thorndike climbed through the hatch onto the bridge of the CGS *Willow Star*. He felt a wave of irritation at the sight of the alien graveyard displayed on the viewscreen. His crew had developed a morbid obsession with that graveyard since landing on this planet a week ago, and he was fed up with it.

It's gruesome. Unhealthy.

"Morning, Captain," said Lieutenant Wiley, the lone member on the bridge's skeleton shift this morning.

Thorndike grunted something he hoped would be taken for a greeting as he crossed to the control panel and blanked the screen.

"Anything to report from the night watch?" he asked.

"Not a thing. It's been quiet as a grave out there."

Thorndike shot a quick glare at Wiley, who had turned back to his station, chuckling. His irritation flared again when he noticed Wiley's Bible tucked in the chair beside him.

"Have you been arguing theology with the Utlenders again?"

Wiley swiveled around, his face animated. "Not arguing. Agreeing. It's amazing how similar their *helig rull* is to our Old Testament. The creation account, for inst—"

"I'm really not interested," Thorndike said quickly, forestalling another of Wiley's tiresome discourses on the holy writings of the Utlenders. "What time is our meeting with them this morning?"

"In two hours, sir."

"Good enough. I'm going to check in with Engineering and then grab something to eat."

As he lowered himself through the hatch he saw Wiley press a contact on his panel, and the screen once again displayed a view of the graveyard. Gritting his teeth, he left the bridge without a word.

The meeting pavilion had become familiar in the week since the *Willow Star's* landing on Utlend. Thorndike selected a cushion near one end of the table in the open-air hut across from Ambassador Mischa, the leader of the Utlend delegation. He stretched his legs before him, his ankles turned at an awkward angle beneath the surface of the low table, and envied the way Commander Ashida sank easily into a cross-legged position beside him. His First Officer managed to look graceful despite her gray Consolidated Galaxies uniform.

"*Vi mottar I dag.*" The Ambassador paused for the translator on the table between them to provide the Earther equivalent. "Welcome this beautiful morning."

The Utlender spread his arms wide to acknowledge the lush garden surrounding the pavilion. It *was* a beautiful morning, Thorndike realized, with sunlight filtering through brilliant green leaves and the subtle scent of lilies floating toward them on a gentle breeze. He had been so focused on the upcoming meeting during his walk from the ship that he had missed the birdsong drifting down from the highest branches of the trees that towered over the path.

"Thank you," Thorndike said, then delivered his news. "As you requested, we placed a satellite in orbit last night. The recording equipment is fully functional."

A squeal of gibberish erupted from the translator between them, and the Ambassador responded in kind.

"Excellent!" the translator intoned. "Then you will record our Great Journey so all the worlds can see the glory of God."

Thorndike managed not to react as Mischa exchanged smiles with the half-dozen Utlenders sitting on his side of the table. Their expressions were amazingly similar to humans, unlike some of the alien races belonging to the Consolidated Galaxies. Their bodies, too, were humanoid, with two arms and two legs and similar facial features. Their heads were larger, though; covert analysis had revealed expanded brainpans and an amazing amount of synaptic activity, indicating intelligence far in advance of any human.

If these Utlenders are so intelligent, Thorndike wondered, *then why are they so technologically backward? They're too focused on their religion, and not enough on advancement.*

Beside him, Ashida leaned forward and spoke to Rouvin, Ambassador Mischa's second. "We've got viewcams set up at the graveyard too, as you instructed. We're ready to start recording whenever you give the word."

"Soon, soon," Rouvin responded. "Tomorrow after the second meal, when we will make feast to honor God for sustaining us in this place."

Thorndike set his teeth in frustration. He had heard more about God in the past week than in his whole life. It seemed to him that these aliens could talk about nothing else, as though the *Willow Star* had landed in the middle of a monastery or something. Several of the crew, like Wiley and even Ashida, were thrilled. But they were religious, and he, most definitely, was not.

His mind skipped back thirty years. He was fifteen, scrunched down in the back pew of the church. The preacher stood at the front of the sanctuary, talking about sin and forgiveness and other church buzzwords. Beside him, his best friend Jake leaned over and whispered, "This crap is for weak-minded idiots who don't know how to take their lives into their own hands." Jake made more sense than the preacher, to Thorndike's way of thinking.

Across the table, Ambassador Mischa nodded. "You are, of course, invited to join us for the meal, and to bring your crew. We will feast until the time for our Great Journey."

Forcing a smile, Thorndike said, "We wouldn't miss it."

Rouvin caught him in a direct gaze. "We have been reading your Holy Bible, Captain Thorndike and we have many questions. For instance, who are the two witnesses giving testimony in the mystic city.?"

Thorndike shook his head. "That's really not my area of expertise. Ashida here might be able to help you. You can ask me about FTL travel, or spaceships, or even ancient Earthy history, but I don't know anything about religion."

Rouvin and Mischa exchanged a glance, their faces carefully impassive.

"Most regrettable, your lack of knowledge," Mischa said, and though the words the translator provided were devoid of emotion, the alien's voice was full of it. "We understand that were it not for your ignorance, you could not have been sent here. Your role is important, but we are sorry."

Stinging at being labeled ignorant, Thorndike fought to stay calm. He was on a diplomatic mission, after all. He was here to extend an olive branch to an alien race; if they took that branch and whacked him over the head with it, his job was to endure the beating with a smile.

Rouvin turned to the First Officer. "In the section called 'Revelation' there are many statements that correspond to writings of our *Forutsi*..." When the translator failed to supply an Earther equivalent, he tried a different word. "Our predictors of holy events."

"Prophets," said Ashida.

Rouvin nodded. "I am excited to compare those similarities with you. We can do that now?"

Before Ashida could answer, Thorndike drew his legs from beneath the table and got awkwardly to his feet. "I think I'll go check on the science team," he said, wanting nothing more than to escape before a detailed Bible discussion got underway. "Maybe I'll send Wiley to take my place here."

Ashida gave him a grateful look while Ambassador Mischa nodded. "Lieutenant Wiley is most knowledgeable in these matters."

Thorndike struggled to maintain a tranquil expression. "I'm sure he is."

A soft knock on his cabin door interrupted Thorndike's task of recording the day's events into his journal.

"Come in," he called as he tapped the touchscreen on his desk.

Ashida and Wiley stepped inside the cramped cabin.

"Do you have a minute, sir?" Ashida asked.

He gestured to indicate they should sit on the bunk, and swiveled his chair around to face them.

"We wanted to tell you about our discussions with the Utlenders today," Wiley said. The comm officer looked tired and in need of a shave.

"When was the last time you slept, Lieutenant?"

"I was just getting ready to do that, sir," the younger man replied. "But this is important, so I wanted to talk to you first."

Thorndike rocked back in his chair. "I'm listening."

Wiley looked at Shida, who nodded for him to proceed. "Rouvin introduced us to some of their holy men today, the ones who have been studying the copy of the Bible we gave them. It's amazing, sir, how many similarities they've found to their own holy writings."

"You told me that this morning," Thorndike said. "But I can't understand why they're spending so much time on a book of religion instead of the scientific information we've shared with them."

"It's their way of life, sir," Wiley answered. "Their religion *is* their way of life. But what they told us today is pretty amazing. It's not just that many of our Biblical prophecies match up with theirs, it's that theirs clarify ours. They showed us a detailed interpretation of Daniel's seventy sevens, for instance. And they have one that matches most of the book of Revelation passage for passage, only theirs is so clear. It's almost as if we were given the symbols and they were given the key."

As Wiley's voice grew louder with excitement, Thorndike's irritation level rose. He took a deep breath. He didn't want to lose his temper with a junior officer.

"Is there a point to this?"

Wiley glanced at Ashida before continuing. "Yes, sir. After our discussions today, we believe their Great Journey tomorrow is directly connected to prophecies in our Bible."

Thorndike pursed his lips, balancing his chin on steepled fingertips. "Let me get this straight. You believe the religious practices of an alien race will have an effect on Earth, which is thousands of light years away."

The two on the bunk exchanged a glance before Ashida answered. "If what we saw today is true, then the Utlenders' Great Journey will trigger an event called the Rapture on Earth. Christians believe that's when Jesus will come back and—"

"I know what the Rapture is," Thorndike interrupted, trying hard to keep the condescension out of his voice. From the abashed look on Ashida's face, he didn't succeed. "Okay, suppose you're right and the Utlenders have a Rapture-like prophecy too. Isn't it supposed to be a surprise? No one knows when it will happen. Isn't that part of the whole 'watch the skies for the end is near' thing?"

She leaned forward, a strand of dark hair drifting at the side of her face where it had come loose from the knot at the back of her head. "Not on Earth, maybe, but Earth is a fallen world. Utlend isn't. Haven't you noticed how like paradise this planet is? It's like our Garden of Eden. And the Utlenders live thousands of years, not a few decades like we do. They would probably live forever if the sin of the first humans hadn't introduced physical decay into their universe."

Thorndike stared at Ashida, astounded that the normally level-headed officer actually seemed to believe this stuff. He didn't even know how to answer such a preposterous statement.

Wiley suddenly burst out in a loud voice, "If you know what the Rapture is, then you know what will happen if you don't accept Christ before it occurs. There's still time to reconsider, sir."

Thorndike turned an incredulous glare on him. "Are you trying to convert *me*?"

Wiley met his gaze head-on. "If at all possible, sir."

Caught in the younger man's earnest stare, Thorndike paused. Wiley really believed what he was saying, and apparently so did Ashida. What if there was something to this Christian stuff after all?

Then Thorndike shook his head. As Jake had said all those years ago, these two were nothing but a pair of weak-minded idiots. And insolent, too. Imagine, trying to convert their Captain.

His temper flared as Ashida spoke again. "Captain, if we're right, we have to notify Earth. Millions of Christians will want to know."

Thorndike didn't bother to keep the derision out of his voice at such an outrageous suggestion. "If you expect me to contact Earth and tell them the end of the world is at hand, you've lost your mind." He looked first Ashida and then Wiley directly in the eye. "What has gotten into you two? You're both officers, and scientists. We're here to make diplomatic contact with Utlend, period. If you can't keep your personal religious beliefs from clouding your professional judgment, I'll relieve you of duty and have you both confined to quarters. Is that clear?"

They both nodded, subdued, and Ashieda whispered, "Yes, sir."

"Good. Then you're dismissed." As they opened the cabin door, Thorndike stopped them. "Oh, and one more thing. Do not send a message to Earth, not even a personal one. That's a direct order."

Judging by the disappointment in Wiley's eyes, Thorndike knew he had intended to do just that. But both officers nodded, and he turned back to his work as the door closed softly behind them.

Thorndike managed to miss the feast the next day by assigning himself as senior officer for the skeleton crew that remained aboard the *Willow Star*. After a restless night filled with disturbing dreams, he had no patience to sit through the Utlenders' religious ramblings. Instead, he and Ensign Haywood spent the afternoon running final checks on the recording equipment focused on the alien graveyard.

The sight of the sepulcher Ambassador Mischa had identified as belonging to the first Utlender—Utlend's version of Adam, Thorndike supposed—filled the screen. Its rounded stone walls had been carefully sanded smooth and its surface engraved with alien markings similar to the ancient hieroglyphics Thorndike had studied at university. Even the enormous tombstone-shaped rock that blocked the entrance was covered with intricate engravings, making it the most ornate burial place he had ever seen. It gave him the creeps.

"I'll be glad when this is over and we can get back to business with the Utlenders," he told Haywood.

"Yes, sir," the young Ensign answered, his eyes on the instrument panel before him. "The feast must be over. Here comes the crew."

"About time," Thorndike muttered, turning to watch as his bridge officers climbed through the hatch. The rest of the twelve-member crew followed, lining the back wall to get a good view of the screen. He carefully avoided the gazes of Ashida and Wiley, not yet ready to forgive them for their nonsense of last night. Let them stew awhile, wondering if they had ruined their reputations with a CG superior officer.

"Everything's ready to go," Haywood told Wiley as he surrendered the comm chair and shifted to the next station to man the viewcam controls.

"Sorry you missed it, Sam," Wiley told the Ensighn. "The food was great. There's leftovers in the mess when you get a chance."

"Looks like the show's about to start," Haywood said, nodding toward the screen.

Shifting his gaze, Thorndike saw a small delegation come into view. He thought he recognized Ambassador Mischa, but none of the others looked familiar. They stepped around burial mounds and arranged themselves in a semi-circle before the sepulcher upon which the viewcam was focused, then knelt.

"A shame we don't have sound there," remarked Wiley, his eyes fixed on the screen. "I'd love to hear their prayer."

Thorndike clamped his jaw shut, thankful that their only mikes were attached to the viewcam installed high in the treetops on the edge of the graveyard and weren't powerful enough to pick up the sounds of the prayer.

After a few moments the delegation on the screen stood and withdrew, their mouths moving in unison in what Thorndike guessed was some sort of chant.

"Switch to satellite view," ordered Ashida from where she stood behind the navigator's station, her hand resting on the back of his chair.

The view on the screen changed to a wide-angle shot of the graveyard thirty-five kilometers away. From here they could see the whole thing, thousands of burial mounds in a wide-open field that must have been five kilometers around. Thorndike saw the sepulcher as a tiny structure in the center with small figures the size of insects walking away from it.

Haywood gave a low whistle. "Man-oh-man, look at all those aliens!"

Thousands of them, hundreds of thousands maybe, stood dozens deep in a ring around the perimeter of the graveyard. The sheer number of Utlenders participating in this religious ceremony was astounding.

"It almost looks like everyone on the planet is out there," Thorndike said, shaking his head.

Wiley threw him an odd look. "They are."

Thorndike's head jerked toward the lieutenant. "All of them?"

Wiley nodded. "It's the Great Journey of their entire race. Every living Utlender will go."

Thorndike looked back toward the screen, interested in spite of himself. "So what happens now?"

"I think they're all praying," Wiley said. "Let's see if we can hear anything yet."

He pressed a contact to activate the audio, and an eerie sound filled the bridge. Thorndike felt the hair on his scalp prickle as the haunting sound of thousands of alien voices joined together in song reached his ears. Harmonies no human had ever heard cascaded up and down the melody, filling him with a sense of wonder, as though in a deeply hidden recess of his soul he knew the meaning of the words he didn't understand.

On the screen, the Utlenders all lifted their arms, reaching high into the air as their song ended abruptly, followed by an eerie silence. Thorndike's stomach muscles tightened as a sense of expectation became almost palatable on the bridge of the *Willow Star*.

Suddenly a loud *pop!* Echoed through the speakers.

"What was that?" asked Haywood.

Ashida crossed to the science station behind the command chair and tapped a query into the keyboard. She looked up at Thorndike, her eyes wide.

"That was a P-wave. We're having an earthquake. And the focal depth looks like it's almost six thousand kilometers."

Thorndike shook his head. "That's impossible. There must be something wrong with the instruments. That would be all the way to the planet's core. Where's the epicenter?"

She raised her head and fixed her gaze on the screen. "Right there. At the center of the graveyard."

Everyone looked up when the first S-wave hit. With a gigantic shake, the ground split in front of the sepulcher and a deep narrow chasm opened directly before it. The surface waves followed quickly after, causing the ground on the screen to appear to roll as the burial mounds shifted like floats on a billowing ocean. Thousands of Utlenders staggered with the movement, but Thorndike didn't see any of them fall. After one gigantic roll, the scene grew still for a moment, and then a second wave started, this one too seeming to generate outward from the chasm in the center of the graveyard.

"Brace yourself," advised Ashida.

Moments later the deck gave a violent shudder as the first surface wave reached the ship at the same time the graveyard, thirty-five kilometers away, rolled with the second. The crew lining the rear of the bridge pitched and grabbed at one another for support. Fascinated, Thorndike clutched the arms of his chair, his eyes riveted on the viewscreen and the burial mounds shifting beneath the ground. They vibrated, every one of them, until all at once they burst open. With a showering of rich, brown soil, the mounds erupted like thousands of mini volcanos. Behind them several of the crew gasped.

"Would you look at that," said Ashida, her low voice full of awe.

Thorndike couldn't have spoken if he wanted to. He was dimly aware that beside him Wiley prayed quietly, but he could not tear his eyes away from the screen, for out of the burial mounds came movement. Living Utlenders rose from the dirt.

"Let's see it up close," Ashida whispered, and Haywood adjusted the view to focus on one small patch of ground where a dozen or so of the aliens stepped from the freshly churned earth, all of them lifting their hands, their heads thrown back and their mouths moving as they shouted toward the sky.

As one, they turned and began walking toward the center of the graveyard. Without being told, Haywood shifted the view to the tomb. Just as the viewcam focused, an aftershock shook the ground. The massive stone blocking the entrance to the sepulcher shuddered violently, then toppled forward. It slammed onto the ground across the chasm, forming a bridge over the gaping hole in the planet's crust. Blinding light shot from the entrance to the tomb, so bright the ship's emergency filters kicked in, and the screen went black.

"Get it back," Thorndike shouted, appalled to hear the panic that had gripped him deep inside echoing in his voice.

Haywood's hands flew over the instrument panel and in moments the screen once again displayed the tomb. Thousands of Utlenders lined up before it, the column reaching beyond the viewcam's focus. As Thorndike watched, slack-jawed, they marched across the makeshift bridge one by one and disappeared into the blinding brightness of the tomb.

Thorndike barked an order as he whirled around in his chair. "Get a reading on that-"

He stopped. The science station was empty. He twisted sideways toward the comm station. It was empty also. Ashida and Wiley were both gone.

From his position beyond Wiley's empty chair, Haywood stared at him, his face white with shock. "He just disappeared! I was looking right at him, and he vanished!"

Icy dread gripped Thorndike's gut, and his heart thumped loudly in his ears. His hands dripped sweat on the arms of the command chair as he swallowed against a throat gone suddenly dry. *It was true.* Wiley and Ashida had tried to warn him. They had recognized the evidence.

He heard someone sobbing quietly behind him as he raised his eyes to the screen. One by one the Utlenders disappeared into the tomb on their Great Journey to... where? The same place Ashida and Wiley had gone? And were millions on Earth gone there as well?

Thorndike rubbed his brow as understanding dawned. His role was important, as Ambassador Misha had told him plainly. Because of his ignorance, he would take a recording back to Earth. Because of his ignorance, he was still here to do it.

"Symbols and Keys" originally appeared in *Dragons, Knights, and Angels* magazine, June 2004

The Repair Blessing

Mark Francis

"Howbeit when he, the Spirit of truth, is come, he will guide you into all truth: for he shall not speak of himself; but whatsoever he shall hear that shall he speak: and he will shew you things to come." (John 16:13)

"God, is that you?" I silently wondered. My family and I had just enjoyed a lunch date at our favorite restaurant. As I wrote the check to cover our meal and tip, I felt a gentle nudge to give an additional amount to our waitress as a blessing.

Still unsure, I shared the thought with my wife. After considering for a moment, she too felt we were being led. I quickly wrote a short note of encouragement and left it with the extra blessing. On the way home, we asked God to make His love real to her.

The next morning, I left for the same restaurant to meet with a friend for breakfast. Arriving early to read, I was given a table in the quiet, but empty back section. Absorbed in my book, I hadn't noticed the same waitress who had served us the day before filling salt and pepper shakers on each table. She appeared tentative and finally approached where I sat.

Almost embarrassed, she shared her story. Before work the day before, her car had broken down and she didn't know how she would cover the repairs. With tears filling her eyes, she told me the extra blessing we left for her at lunch was the *exact* amount the repairs required!

We expect God's direction and leading in the big things of our lives. But when we receive His encouragement for doing the small but outrageous, anything can happen!

Vanquished Dread

Teresa Hanly

In my recent experiences with the death and illnesses of family and friends, I experienced my own brush with death and open-heart surgery.

I didn't know where to "put" God, if putting Him in the middle of it meant He was putting His signature on the suffering that had come into my life.

I underwent nine hours of surgery, while heart and lung machines were keeping me alive. Closely monitored for nine days more, I lay in ICU, feeling put back together like a Raggedy Ann doll. I had so many painful places where tubes were running through my body. And by my bedside, noisy monitors were detecting signs of life.

"I can't talk to Him," I whispered to myself. Where dread had filled my soul, no prayer could be uttered. Then my husband came in the room and set up the iPod so my favorite songs and hymns would fill the air. Though my body could hardly shed a tear, my soul wept. Soon the voice of Him who loves me most broke through my fearful heart, touching deep within. I felt Him right beside me in the darkness, where dread disabled.

He gave me songs of faith to utter, when I had no strength or will to do it. And my heart has its reasons to live, and the faith that seemed buried, declared itself to me. Yes, I hope in God! I am His, and He is mine! I will rise!

Cowboy

Sam Wilson

Those old cows won't mean too much to anyone else. When that truck pulled up to haul them away, this cowboy got a lump in his throat big enough to choke a horse.

You get attached to those critters when you raise them from calves and feed them twice a day. Knowing they won't be back is hard for me to take.

These herd cows are different from feeder cattle. You keep them for years and know each one of them individually.

Selling these cows will fend off the bank for one more year. With a job downtown and someone to lease the range, I'll be able to feed the wife and kids for another year.

Nigh on to three years ago I had to see to the sheep herd. I've worked with sheep since I was knee high to a grasshopper.

One of my jobs when I was a kid was to feed the orphaned lambs and the lambs the ewes could not feed. With a pop bottle, a nipple on it, and a little milk, I became their surrogate mother.

So when I had to sell the herd my heart cried for the longest time, but a man's got to do what a man's got to do.

I guess I could sell the horses and ole Topper out in the corral, but with the years and the miles that they have on them, they're as broken down as I am.

Some of the best times in this old cowboy's life have been spent on Toppy's back, running down some rank old steer or just riding up country for a look-see.

Times are changing. The money boys are taking over. Shoot, even the Chinese are getting in the game. I guess this kind of life for these small ranchers is dern near gone. It won't be long 'til everything is grown on corporate ranches and farms.

What a sad ending to a wonderful way of life.

New Life from Death

Mark Francis

"O Lord, thou hast searched me, and known me." (Psalm 139:1)

"I'm sorry Mark, but we have to cut you from the team." The finality of his statement stabbed my heart like a piercing sword. I stood shocked.

Since junior high school, I had always seen myself playing college football. Year after year, I honed my skills, grew stronger, and distinguished myself on and off the field. Finally, in the spring of my senior year, *the* letter arrived. Texas A&M University had invited me to their summer training camp. Overjoyed, the dream that had motivated every workout came alive.

But now, on the first day of camp, the head trainer was cutting me loose. My physical had revealed some potential for further harm in my shoulder. Unfortunately, as a non-scholarship recruit, the coaches felt I posed too great a financial risk if I became injured. I pleaded for any chance to play, but to no avail. In a moment, all my years of work, sweat and faithful hope died. I was devastated.

For months afterward, I agonized over my long held aspirations. But with great tenderness, God slowly began to open my eyes to see myself in brand new ways. I discovered there was more to me than just athletics. His revealing insight had uncovered other desires I had long been blind to.

The temptation to settle for less than we really are taunts us unceasingly. However, whether in our successes or failures, only God can bring us to our true selves where dreams and destiny can become one.

Making Room for Memories

Penelope Burbank

When my youngest of five sons died at the age of three, I tried to bring order to my life as I dealt with the grief. Shock and denial gave way to confusing anger. Since that was more than I could deal with, I boxed it up and stored it in the basement of my mind.

Storing the hurt and pain that was beyond my personal comprehension was not a conscious choice. Also, I did not realize how those pent-up emotions blocked life from flowing freely through me.

As the years continued, I accumulated many material items in a concrete storage unit. I could not stand to part with the most insignificant objects because of the memories attached to each one; a broken basinet, faded baby clothes, and deserted toys. The time, energy, and cost of saving all those unnecessary items diminished the quality of my life. That was when I learned a valuable lesson about both material and emotional clutter and the negative effect they had on living freely.

One day, as I was digging through the boxes in storage for a greatly needed item, I realized how unmanageable my life had become. It was time to tackle the disorder in the rented unit, no matter how unpleasant and difficult it would be.

During the process of ridding objects from my life, I discovered that I also had to deal with the pent-up turmoil from losing my tender little son. The years had turned my grief to bitterness and it marred all of my other relationships.

Those disturbing thoughts came to me as I worked through piles of cherished childhood treasures that were mixed with tarnished antiques. The items were intertwined like the threads of a tapestry. As I sorted through them, I wondered, *What should I discard? What should I keep?*

During the purge, I came across a bag of incomplete crafts. Among them I found several abandoned embroidery projects. Turning one of them over in my hands, I saw only the loose threads and knots. That view obscured the beauty of the almost finished piece of art.

In that moment I realized my perception of life was twisted with unresolved grief like the mass of knots and loose threads on that unfinished tapestry. I was unable to see the beauty in my life through the boxed-up resentment over my young son's death.

For years, I had been going through the daily actions of life by trying to meet expectations with accomplishments marked off a long list. Perfectionism was my way of looking good on the outside despite being torn and broken on the inside.

Thus, my mind was as cluttered and disorganized as the storage unit. I could not access a happy memory for fear of toppling a sad one. Therefore, I thought it was better to keep the large *mental* door closed and padlocked.

Realizing I was living in the shadow of my son's death brought me to a place of new resolve. Forcing myself to clear the wreckage stored in my mind took extreme amounts of conscious effort and patience. As I let go of the years of emotional build-up, a miraculous thing happened. Each time I allowed myself to experience sorrow; it created room for blocked joyful memories to be renewed. Instead of seeing only the knots of anguish and loose threads of a life lost too soon, I started to see how other memories interconnected to form the landscape of our loving relationship. I gradually visualized the tapestry of my little son and his short life from a different perspective.

Mental images started to flow more freely. My little blond-haired boy with bright blue eyes stood before me with his tattered blanket around his shoulders waiting for me to draw him into my loving embrace. His wide smile appeared as his innocent little voice echoed in my mind, "Rock me, Mommy." And the image of our playful bedtime ritual, which always ended with his sweet, "Mommy, I love you!" soothed my heart.

Today, I know that nothing can completely take away the sorrow of losing my beloved child. However, I once again live with the joyful memories of the three precious years I had with David. Finally, I am able to look upon our shared life, not as an unfinished project, but as a delightful tapestry.

Mirror Images

Teresa Hanly

Looking through the looking glass
My reflection did I see
And gazing on, great darkness
The sin sick world in me

Digging through the darkened pool
Of memories I would find
Wrongs that were done by others
Revealed my own guilt to my mind

I wrestled with this heavy load
And all throughout the night
Knowing that my only hope
Was to bring them to the Light

I stood and watched so desperately
My deeds laid open bare
And gazing on the brightest Light
Dissolved all that was there

My shame and guilt had vanished
A slave of sin set free
This sinner found her Savior
Now I am free indeed

Looking through the looking glass
My reflection do I see
And gazing on, Love's face divine
And the Blood that was shed for me

The Book of Your Heart

Virginia Smith

Putting up the Christmas tree at my house is a very special event. I relish the ritual of hanging the ornaments I've collected over the years. Each one holds a memory. The shiny silver bell engraved with our wedding date. The brightly painted teddy bear with the year of my daughter's birth painted on his hat. The skiing Santa I bought on our first ski trip. As I lift each treasure carefully out of the box where it has lain hidden from view all year, a precious memory emerges from deep within my heart and finds a place on my tree.

I imagine stories are like those ornaments, each one a treasure nestled within the heart of a writer, waiting to be brought out and displayed. Perhaps that's how we first recognize that we are fiction writers: fictitious people walk and talk and breathe within us, and we burn with the desire to show them to others. A story unfolds with startling clarity in our minds, and we know—just know—that we won't have a moment's peace until we've set it down on paper and shared it.

That burning desire is exactly what enables us to tell a story that stirs the imaginations of others. It is our passion for the story and the characters that causes us to spend hours striving for the precise word or the perfect phrase to relay the vivid images in our heads. For some, the stories conceived in our hearts burst from us full-grown; others hold a story inside, nurturing it in the deep places until it ripens into the thing of beauty we've envisioned.

Many years ago, a story bloomed in my heart. It was full of adventure and love, and infused with hope—truly, a thing of beauty. I wrote the first draft feverishly, the words pouring onto the page as the plot unfolded in my mind. The characters were so real, their struggles painful and vivid. I studied the craft, intent on telling my tale with artistry. With each new skill I learned, I revised and polished until the story sparkled. If ever a story was born from the heart, it was that one.

Unfortunately, I couldn't find an editor who shared my passion. Whether due to my lack of skill or the uncertainties of the market for that genre, the story of my heart was rejected over and over. I mourned. I raged. I cried out to God, "Why did You give me this story if You don't intend me to tell it?" After my rage died, I revised and polished the manuscript again. Finally, when there was not a single word that hadn't been scrubbed until it shone, I gave up. After all, if there was no place for the story of my heart in the publishing world, maybe there was no place for me there either.

That's when I heard God's whisper: *Do you think I have only one story to give?*

A few days later, a character waltzed into my mind and began telling me about her life. She became real to me, as real as the characters in my first story. I discovered that there was room in my heart for her, too. In fact, this new tale took on a glimmer and shine all its own. I employed the skills I'd honed on my first, and eventually, God placed a published book in my hands.

And then He said: *I have more stories to give you.*

Can you imagine anything sadder than a Christmas tree with only a single ornament? Or a life with only a single precious memory? Or a heart with only a single story?

I am convinced that good stories are born in the heart of God, a heart immense and overflowing with creativity. He carefully selects an author for each one and bestows a precious gift–straight from His heart to ours. We write it and polish it and, when the story has become as beautiful as we can make it, we must hang it on the tree and reach into the box for another treasure.

"The Book of your Heart" originally appeared in *Christian Fiction Online Magazine,* December 2008

A Mundane Epiphany

Julie Turvey Scott

The day unravels by 7:45am. I take my car to the shop and walk the mile-plus distance home. That's fine. I need the exercise. Once inside, I intend to spend my quiet time reading God's Word. Too often my days don't demonstrate to the Lord the priority I claim to give to Him.

Psalm 15 describes people who are at home in the presence of God. "How do I measure up?" I ask myself. Knowing it's not possible to change the rest of my life, I write in my journal, "Lord, *today* I give you my thoughts, actions, responses, and plans."

My daughter needs to enroll in a college class, and then she wants us to do a little bride-to-be shopping. I inform her that she can have a part of my day, but a significant chunk of my time must include my seat being firmly planted in front of my computer, working. She rolls her eyes but doesn't say anything. She thinks the computer owns me. Or that I am a poor steward of my time. Or both. I concede, "I can shop for an hour after your registration, but I can't spend the whole day, okay?" Ninety-five degrees of sunshine blazes through the windows of her un-air-conditioned car, but a cloud hangs between us.

Community colleges are government entities. Paperwork and hoops to jump through. We return home to locate specific documentation from the past three years. Gasp! My piling, uh, filing system smirks at me, harboring a needed tax form. My pulse races and I substitute a document I hope will be acceptable. I hate panic mode.

Bethany, our paperwork, a darker cloud, and I rush back to her car. She feels responsible for taking my time—I can feel it. She can feel it. This second trip to the city can't be helped. I silently call on the Lord for grace.

BLING!

A mundane epiphany occurs. I turn to Bethany and smile. "I guess *this* is how God wanted to spend His day, because I gave it to Him this morning!"

She smiles in return. "Thank you, Mom."

The cloud has lifted, even though the day continues on the hazy detour. I may not know where I am going, but I know Who does.

Prayer For My Time Management Journey

Jim Thacher

From Dr. Luke's book what Jesus said I learn.
Time management truths I daily must discern.
For each job I commit to both people and to task
To fulfill each in balance, Lord, this is what I ask:
May future events shape my present timely goal.
By planning ahead, my future builds my soul.
May I show God's love to Him and fellow man
And at decision points, choose the best I can.
My time is not my own but filled with work or play
Its use is known by God, every hour of every day.
My focus and my goals, priorities, assets too.
My relationships and roles, God's glory must pursue.
To correct what displeases Him, to plan, to delegate, to lead,
Guided only by Him, this is my urgent need.
God's my Master and my Lord, steward am I to Him,
Accountable to His Word, This is my prayer for Jim.

Why Come to Church?

Jim Cook

Some of the greatest pleasure we get out of life comes from things we do together with other people. A ball game. A theater event or concert. A party. A dinner. Some people even find it very hard ever to do things alone.

Enjoying God is not something we were meant to do in a vacuum. It can be very private. But it can also be a group activity.

We so often think of worship as a solemn event. In fact, worshipers frequently look like mourners!

Worship is not meant to be a duty to be performed every Sunday. It is not a task to be accomplished.

Worship is a time of celebration! Corporate worship is a time to get together with others and revel in the glories of our God! It is a time to be thrilled by Who He is and what He is doing. It is a time to get excited!

Instead of sitting solemnly through a litany of hymns and scripture and exhortation, we should be hardly able to contain ourselves because of the sheer pleasure of knowing our God and His wonders.

The various parts of the worship service should be nothing more than devices to aid us in focusing our worship:

- The hymns are a means of expressing our mutual admiration and praise and joy together with a single voice. David said to make a "joyful" noise! (Psalm 100:1a)

- The prayer time is a chance to speak to our Friend and our Loved One all at once with mutual delight
- The offering is simply a time to say "Thank you" to the One whose "grace has no measure," whose power "has no boundaries known unto man, for out of His infinite riches in Jesus, He giveth and giveth, and giveth again!" (Annie Johnson Flint)
- The Bible reading is a time to listen together to what our Loved One has to say. It is a chance to focus together on the same thoughts, to be "on the same wavelength," both with Him and with each other
- The sermon is an opportunity to learn together and to grow together. We should approach it eagerly, expecting to find out something new about the One who already excites us!
- Baptismal services are a chance to welcome new additions to the family as they identify themselves with Christ. These are times of special celebration
- Communion services are a moment in which to reflect with awe on the love that our God has for us, that He would permit His beloved Son to endure the unimaginable agony of the cross, and even more the separation between Father and Son, just in order to make it possible for us to be part of the family. Such moments can only make our enjoyment of Him the greater
- Testimonies and missionary reports are an opportunity to rejoice in what God is doing

The worship service is more than just the sum of its parts, though. Corporate worship is a time to share our experiences with others, talking about our mutual Lover. It is a time to bolster each other up with words and deeds of encouragement and aid. It is a time to present a united front to Satan.

Anyone who thinks that attending church is dull has failed to understand the concept of corporate worship. Worship should affect us almost as though we were having a party! It should be a time of pleasurable emotion, a time of buoyed hopes, of refreshment and contentment. How can we stand missing such an opportunity! It should be as essential as bread and water!

And best of all, it is a time to get together with our God without distraction. It's a family time! A group time. And He is there!

> Matthew 18:20—"For where two or three come together in my name, there am I with them."

The early Church didn't meet together every week. They met together every day, hours upon end. They encouraged each other. They shared with each other. They fellowshipped with God and each other.

Worship services in previous centuries, even early into the twentieth century, lasted all day, sometimes for several days. It is only in our society of false priorities that we have trouble squeezing out an hour for the One we love!

Corporate worship is one of the greatest gifts God has given us. *Our worship is not a do-it-yourself project. It is a come-as-you-are party!*

Secrets in Her Pockets

Peggy Bert

She returned home to the familiar four rooms on the second floor of the family's rented flat, more crowded now than when she left. Mom, Dad and brother lived here; now an uncle and cousin, too. Would six people all inhabit this small space? What was going on? What had happened while she was away?

It was almost three years ago that she left home. She announced that she was entering the convent at age twelve, fresh out of the eighth grade. Her mother was proud; her father was troubled over it. Their beautiful daughter was a strong-willed child who usually got her way. She made it clear that going into the convent was her assignment direct from God. Now, who should question that?

In those days, young girls entering the convent would immediately become a "postulant" (candidate) for that religious order of nuns. They were clothed in long-sleeved, ankle-length, black garb with unique head coverings to designate their candidacy. After one year, they were elevated to "novice" status. The novitiate was a period of probation before taking the final sacred vows that made an affiliation permanent and perpetually binding.

Adele's enthusiasm for her perceived "calling" began to diminish. Most meals consisted of bread and lard, with broth or tea. On rare occasions, there was meat – but the type was not easily recognizable. She had to wax the expansive convent floors by hand, with candle wax, along with other daily, physically taxing chores. There was no contact with the outside world. No news, no radio, no letters or phone calls —very lonely for a girl of twelve. The first visiting day with family was six months after entering this strict, secluded environment. Her deep faith and trust in God sustained her in the difficulties of life.

Adele's mother was an accomplished seamstress who made her convent clothing. Learning of her daughter's distress on that first visiting day, she decided to sew a special garment for her. It would look exactly like the original, but it would contain extra-long, below-the knee, wide, deep pockets in each side. On subsequent, now more frequent, visiting days, the family would bring their daughter sandwiches and other goodies that she could conceal in those big secret pockets. The quantities fed her and several other girls. Adele slyly slipped the food to others in the dim, candle-lit chapel at evening prayer time or in the shadowy hallways on the way to their rooms for lights out.

This scheme grew to include a "Hot Tamale Street Vendor." Adele received money from her parents to buy the hot tamales – one of her favorite foods. Her father gleefully informed the "Tamale Man" of the clandestine meeting site. A seven-foot, stone wall surrounded the perimeter of the convent. At the designated place, Adele would exchange a whistle signal with him. She threw the money over the wall; he threw over the hot tamales.

Fortified with that extra food, Adele went on to become a novice at the ripe old age of thirteen.

In less than two years, she would take her final vows and become a full-fledged nun. As that day drew near, it was discovered that she had a malignant ovarian tumor. Surgery was scheduled to remove it. The religious order could not be financially responsible for someone who had not yet taken her final vows, and who may experience declining health for many years. They thought it in her best interest to release her unconditionally. Her father was beaming, overjoyed that she was home. It was late 1932–the time of the Great Depression. Our country was deep in the throes of economic disaster. Security in stocks, property and possessions vanished. Many were destitute. Once-reliable banks and companies went broke and closed. Millions lost their jobs. That included Adele's father, brother, uncle and cousin.

Her mother was supporting all of them. As a seamstress, she designed and made clothing for the people who could still afford custom-made, trendy apparel.

After recuperation from surgery, Adele announced early one morning that she was going out to look for a job. This was met with roaring laughter. "There are no jobs; it's the Depression." Everyone tried to explain the situation to her, but she refused to accept the foolishness and futility of what she was about to face. She had been cloistered in a convent with no comprehension of what had gone on.

Adorned in a stylish, sophisticated, stunning outfit, with matching hat, her steps had the bounce and vitality of a woman on a mission.

She reappeared at sunset, having achieved the impossible. She landed a job! The executive secretary to the president of a large shoe manufacturing company urgently needed an assistant secretary.

"But you can't even type," shrieked her mother. "Can you take shorthand?"

"No, but I told them I could!" Adele shot back.

"You'll be fired your first day!" her mother yelled.

"I *can* and *will* do it. You'll see. You won't have to support the family alone anymore."

Her back was to the president's secretary, somewhat concealing her slow peck on the noisy typewriter keys. It was her third day on the job. Suddenly she felt a firm hand grasp her shoulder.

"You don't know how to type, do you, Adele?

"No," she answered.

"Shorthand?"

"No."

She was conscientious and everyone liked her instantly. Instead of being fired, she was sent to school after work, to learn typing and shorthand. Adele became a superb secretary, and was also selected to model the company's elegant shoes for department store buyers. Ten years later, now married, her career at the shoe company ended, when she gave birth to me.

My mother taught me how to sing the ABCs, spell my name, brush my teeth, and read before kindergarten. She showed me how to bake cookies, roll piecrust and dance the polka. From her I received my work ethic—that you should always do more than what you get paid for. She modeled the meaning of loyalty, tenacity, courage and the never-give-up attitude. She instilled in me solid moral values of right and wrong; the idea that you can rise above your circumstances, shoot for a goal and go on to achieve it. Mom was the most influential person in my life. Even though she was a difficult taskmaster, a supreme critic and often impossible to please, she was, nevertheless, also my best friend.

Mom is gone now, but she leaves a lingering legacy that will never die. When things get tough and I feel defeated and want to throw in the towel, it's as if Mom is coaching from the clouds. A voice whispers into my mind. "Don't be discouraged. Have faith in God and the abilities He's given you. Together, you *will* make it through this."

Adele held various jobs throughout her life. She had three more daughters—my precious sisters. They are all extremely successful in their careers. Although we're separated by distance, the telephone and e-mail fills in the miles. When we share stories or difficult days, we leave each other with these words: "Remember whose daughter you are. I love you." We inherited the gift of encouraging words—the priceless present slipped into *our* pockets. Our

Mom and Grand Mom gave us insight into the "secret pockets" of their "soul."

Dad

Sam Wilson

A whisper of wind, a rustling tree, a pleasant scent, just memories.

A gentle heart who once was there, who lived and loved, who always cared.

Someone I could share life's problems with, and who would always understand.

Someone when I needed help would always lend a hand.

Just fond memories until we meet again.

Thanks. I love you, Dad. You'll always be my friend.

Take Heart

Colby Russell Drane

"These things 1 have spoken unto you, that in me ye might have peace. In the world ye shall have tribulation: but be of good cheer; 1 have overcome the world." (John 16:33)

Dear, Christian, are you burdened by worry and doubt? Has the path of life become a place of hardship, anguish and toil? Are you wounded and pierced by grief? Do not fear.

Take heart! For Jesus has "...overcome the world."

So often in life, we, as humans, only see what lies right in front of us. So often we are preoccupied with the pain of our hardship that we tend to forget that these moments are blessings from God intended to better us—not to harm us. Dear Christian, He uses them to shape us, form us, and mold us into the exact object of his service that He can use to further the Kingdom. Countless souls in the Bible have endured hardships brought upon by this world.

None more so than Christ who was "... wounded for our transgressions... bruised for our iniquities: the chastisement of our peace was upon him; and with his stripes we are healed. (Isaiah 53: 5)

Never before in the history of the world has anyone suffered more than Christ. Hours before he carried his cross to Golgotha, he endured spitting, mocking, flogging and maiming. He was marred, and covered in blood. The physical pain he endured was immense, but nothing compared to that moment of separation when he cried out in a loud voice, "...My God, my God, why hast thou forsaken me?" (Matthew 27: 46)

Notice that Jesus says in no uncertain terms that "...In the world ye *shall* have tribulation." It is not a matter of *if* you will face trouble, dear Christian, but *when*. Remember, the creator knows your pain better than anyone else. You are never alone, no matter how difficult the situation.

"My brethren, count it all joy when ye fall into divers temptations; Knowing this, that the trying of your faith worketh patience. But let patience have her perfect work, that ye may be perfect and entire, wanting nothing." (James 1: 2-4)

He has overcome the world, Dear Christian! Take that to heart, and let it dwell in your utmost being. For not only has he overcome the world, he has overcome death itself. Every trial you face is nothing more than a stepping stone through Christ. For we are "...more than conquerors through him that loved us." (Romans 8: 37)

Do not fear this time of testing, Dear Christian. Welcome it. *Embrace it.* March over it with the love that gives us the "...power to tread on serpents and scorpions, and over all the power of the enemy..." (Luke 10: 19) Then and only then will you be able walk in victory, for he will give you the strength to "...walk and, not faint." (Isaiah 40: 31).

God's Stubbornness

Mark Francis

"God—stubborn? " you may be thinking. I know. It sounds strange. Yet, I invite you to explore this possibility with me. Many times we limit this kind of descriptive language to only negative settings. In doing so, I believe we lose a great amount of vividness in trying to capture the always outlandish character of our God. I hope this message will broaden and deepen our hearts.

Our lives each evoke an incredibly strong response from God. Driven by desire too great to measure, His heart continually beats for union with us. Consuming and unending, His passion *for us* forms the DNA of eternity. And not just any eternity —ours!

Heaven knows full well the presence and power of God's heart. Every heavenly creature lives awed and perplexed in its brilliance. No aspect of their existence goes without being engulfed by the tangible cloud of His presence every moment. All they know and experience originates and flows from the core qualities of His unmatched character. However, the vast effect God imparts upon Heaven pales in comparison to His absolute zealousness for humanity.

The continuing saga of God's intense pursuit of our lives leaves us astonished and bewildered. At times, our heart resists His overt intentions disbelieving these desires for us consume His heart. And yet, as we open up and simply accept His generosity, the floodgates of worth, significance and security overwhelm us. As a result, our growing experience of being "at home" with Him abolishes the heart poison of fear, bringing great joy to His heart and ours.

In our personal journeys, God's persistence staggers our minds. His firm and steadfast purpose to draw us close demolishes every obstacle, warning or setback we encounter. He absolutely refuses to let us go alone. True life is relationship that lasts. In other words, God... is... stubborn!

Different isn't it? To think God is stubborn seems wrong. And while we grapple with our disbelief and awkwardness, He keeps being stubborn in His desired influence in our lives. How so? Consider the following wellsprings of His deep longings for you...

• God is unreasonably rigid in His abandoned love for you. Not governed by any level of logic, He loves you beyond every rational limit anyone would expect.

• God forgives our confessed rebellion with head strong swiftness. Immoveable forgiveness, His vehement and demanding answer to every dark accusation against our lives, shines with continual burning intensity.

• God insists, refusing to yield, in providing you a home with Him. Eternity is union with Him, and He is inflexible in defining it any other way.

• God, unyielding in His desire, persistently opens every door of opportunity to us for coming to Him. He demands the best of everything, including Himself, and offers it with repetitive endurance.

• God obstinately presents freedom to each of us, recklessly willing to lay everything He generously offers before our feet for our choosing. Tenacious or enduring relationships are built with a tenacious value for freedom.

What do you think? Can you see His heart in another way? More importantly, can you receive that He is all this and more to you? As you consider these questions, let me paint another picture of God's stubbornness in our lives.

Growing up in Texas (USA), we often experienced dramatic storms of torrential rain. Heavy, rain-filled clouds would roll in with darkening fury, accompanied by turbulent, powerful winds. Sensing what was coming, we would quickly dress, putting on raincoats, boots and hats, all in an effort to stay dry. The violent storm would arrive with fierceness, sheets of rain falling like a continual waterfall. But no matter how well we dressed, we almost always became drenched. Wetness would find its way through the layers of "protection," soaking us through and through.

God's extraordinary and consuming love touches our lives much like the rainstorms in Texas. No matter how well we put up walls or barriers of fear, disbelief or even rebellion, His love finds its way into our lives. Even the very breath of our lives, saturated with His love, continually reminds us of His enduring presence. Outside of ourselves, the diverse circumstances we encounter, good or bad, always bow and make room for God's passionate desire to be with us. Absolutely nothing can diminish or prevent His presence. But, one major detail remains. The choice to receive remains with us.

God stubbornly loves us with trembling intensity. The fire of His heart can never be quenched, and with every day comes another opportunity to experience His stubborn intimacy. Extraordinary and overwhelming, His stubborn love can powerfully transform our lives. We can trade our obstinacy AGAINST Him for obstinacy WITH Him. And in time, we come to find that our hearts are growing with stubbornness like His own... enduring and unreasonable love for Him and those in our lives.

Juice in Jars

Pam Sherburn

Her grip loosened on Sami's hand when she ran to play with the dog. *A typical thing for a four-year old to do,* Alia thought as she turned from her daughter and faced the entry.

She was the first to arrive at the home after her grandmother's death the previous week. Her foot felt like lead when she stepped into the old farmhouse where Granny lived most of her adult life.

But the tick from the grandfather clock beckoned her into the familiar setting and place of fond memories. The corners of her mouth turned up when she stroked the back of the overstuffed chair where Granny used to read nursery rhymes and tell her stories of real-life heroes.

The lump in her throat didn't have a chance to develop when a flicker from the kitchen caught her attention.

She gravitated toward a bottle of juice on the window ledge and her finger danced with glistening beams of sunlight which streamed through the liquid and onto the counter. She grasped the bottle, pulled it to her chest and closed her eyes while the clock announced a new hour. She counted as she moved toward the pantry—one, two three – a chime for each step. Four, five, six, seven. The sound ended as Alia approached the small room, with the juice still in her embrace.

When she opened the door it was as though she pulled the curtain on a stage and walked into a scene from her past. She watched Granny hover over vapor from a kettle—something she saw her grandmother do for hours, even more so when she made juice. Granny squeezed fresh fruit until liquid ran through the strainer. She worked hard so others could easily swallow the nutritious, refreshing drink. Aromas filled the air and the thought of the sweet nectar teased Alia's taste buds.

"The containers need to be clean so the fruit won't be contaminated," Granny explained when Alia asked why she "baked" the bottles in a pan of shallow water in the oven where the steam sterilized them.

She looked at the contents in the room, and reached for a lone jar. She felt the crack along the side, then observed other containers of various sizes and shapes line the shelves—Granny saved any of them with an opening the size of the form-fitting lids. Alia noticed other bottles, with the juice front and center, like soldiers waiting for orders.

From the recess of her memory she could hear her grandfather proclaim, "God approves!" each time a lid popped, a sign pollutants were sealed out and valuable contents preserved. But Granny said, "My cup runneth over," when her task was done. The reference was more than a motto to her, it was a way of life.

The bounty was more than her grandparents could consume before the next crop arrived the following year. But Granny's heart was as big as the abundant harvest. "Some people have needs and I have blessings," she said with simplicity.

As Alia looked down the row of preserved fruit, other people entered the stage – the toothless man at the mission, the women and children at the homeless shelter, beloved neighbors, and of course her family – all recipients of this woman's labor. Their smile was the only payment Granny needed.

Then the spotlight broadened and Alia looked at more recent years. With clear insight she saw how God accepted people. She observed it in the lives of those from the mission where she and her husband served.

More than once she watched people from different walks of life kneel at the conclusion of a chapel service then rise with a testimony of feeling "clean." They opened their hearts and received the flow of life from the sacrificial offering provided for them.

From that moment, those born from above sensed they were under Divine safety, separated from spiritual death and alive forevermore. Alia circled a lid with her thumb. "Preserved in Christ Jesus-" Granny's voice was almost audible as the passage came to mind.

A beam of conviction zeroed in on her life, one filled with questions and doubts—so much so she didn't pass the blessings she knew to her own little girl.

I've felt so alone—no, numb—since my Babe died in the accident last year.

She gripped the shelf in front of her and rested her head on her hands. In time color returned to her white knuckles and love and peace surged through her. She wiped her eyes on her sleeve, and reached for a jar as the clock announced the eighth hour.

"The doggie likes me!" Sami announced as she bounded in the house.

Alia placed her hand on her youngster's back and guided her toward Granny's chair.

Humpty Dumpty move over. My King can put people together again.

"Come here, Sweetheart." Alia pulled Sami close and she snuggled on her mother's lap.

"I want to tell you about containers and their contents," she said as she placed the bottle in front of them. Her joy was full and her child was the first one she wanted to share the overflow with.

She knew Granny wanted it that way, and God approved.

Another Step to Glory

Sam Wilson

Another step to glory each day that I live
Another step to glory each prayer that is prayed
Another step to glory each moment in God's Word
Another step to glory—what a day to look toward:
To see my Master Jesus, who bled and died for me
When I kneel before His nail-pierced feet,
These words He'll say to me:
"Well done, good and faithful servant,
My gift was not in vain.
For now you'll share my home on high,
And here with me you'll reign."

Sheep, Apple Pie and Songs on the Radio

Peggy Bert

My dear sister:

What will you look like? Will you like me? I wondered. This mysterious upcoming event – your birth, filled me with anticipation. Mom would let me feel her big tummy and tell me that you were waiting for just the right time to come out and be with us. She wanted me to help her take care of you, to sing you songs, to hold you, play with you, tell you stories and draw pictures for you and teach you your ABC's. She would take lots of pictures of us together she said. I was four; you would soon be born.

Our wise mother let me know how important I would be as your older sister and to her as a big helper. Whatever she said and the look in her eyes convincingly conveyed that she had enough love in her heart for more than one daughter; and it made me feel even more special because there would now be "two of us."

Then she would take me into the kitchen and start making an apple pie on the oilcloth covered table—and continue talking – exactly about what – I can't recall. She would teach me songs and we would sing together. But what I remember so vividly is all the sights; sounds and smells of the creation of the pie from start to finish. To this day, to handle and feel unbaked pie dough and inhale the aroma of apple pie baking in the oven evokes warm and cherished memories and a feeling of being loved and cared for. Not until recent years, could I pinpoint the origin of those special feelings. It goes back to those special times when we talked about you – before you were even born. So, my dear sister, from the first times I ever heard about you – those are sweet and permanent pictures in my mind.

One morning, Mom gave me an assignment.

"I want you to pick the name for your new baby sister," she said.

"Whatever name you choose – that will be her name. Will you do that?"

My heart felt like it wanted to jump out of my chest! Although only four years old, I was determined to do the best job I could to come up with a wonderful name that Mom (and you) would love. While trying to fall asleep that night, so many names went rolling around in my head. None seemed quite right. When I awoke the next morning, picking your name was the most important thing in my mind. Many days passed and still no name.

It was the 1940's. Our three-foot-high console radio sat in the corner of our dining room.

I spent many hours in front of that radio. Television was just emerging and most homes didn't have one yet. That "big box radio" was our only source of entertainment in those days. In the evenings, I would lay on the floor, with my ear as close to those speakers as I could get. Songs by the Big Bands and their singers would fill the house. I would be singing with them as Mom and Dad danced in the living room. The song "Linda" came through that old radio many times before. I knew all the words by heart and started singing it.

"When I go to sleep, I never count sheep; I count all the charms about Linda."

There were lines in the song about dreams and miracles – and "wanting to get to know Linda."

It also said, "Linda doesn't know I exist."

This was it! It was PERFECT! This song told about a very special girl that had charm and was loved very much. That just had to be you. Now I knew what your name would be! I ran to Mom and with my voice still panting – told her.

"I love it," she exclaimed. "Your new sister Linda will love it, too!"

Mom and Dad kept dancing; I kept singing; and you had your name!

It was exciting to have a new sister. You got beau coups of love and attention. We would talk and sing to you. Mom said you knew what we were saying by our smiles and felt how much we loved you by our singing as we held you close. This was so much better than being the only daughter. We did everything together.

As you got older, Mom dressed us in matching outfits and hats. We looked like matching ruffled lampshades with bows on top. She made us sing together whenever what even looked like an audience appeared. When we were in junior high and high school, I fondly recall all the times we cleaned house to songs on the radio. We turned it up – good and loud – and together we belted out the lyrics with gusto! We had such good times together—through tears and laughter.

This Christmas you are coming to visit. We'll take lots of pictures, count sheep, bake apple pies for our families and sing those songs on the radio as we roll the dough—together. I can't wait. Sisters: A precious gift from God. Memories: Gifts we create for our family and loved ones today. See you at Christmas!

Love, Your Big Sister, Peggy

I Will Be Your Father

Teresa Hanly

As we entered the home, my mother gave me some crayons and pieces of notebook paper and sent me to an adjacent sitting room to busy myself with coloring. A number of men and women were all surrounding the kitchen area. Soon my mother had gathered some women around her, and as they huddled together, I heard some disturbing chatter.

As a traveling salesman, my dad was gone a lot, but it seemed from their conversation that he was not going to be coming home to us anymore. The youngest of five children, I was only 5 years old at the time. I didn't understand. What did this mean?

As I continued coloring, a great feeling of fear gripped me. My little head was trying to comprehend what I just heard, and my heart began to feel a loss for which I had no understanding. While all alone in my confusion, before I could think of running to my mommy for reassurance and comfort, I suddenly felt a strong presence enter the room beside me. I looked around the room, but no one was there. Then I became aware of something like the warmth of a strong embrace surrounding me. Immediately I felt my fears melt away, being replaced with an unfamiliar peace settling down in my heart.

I was so moved by what I experienced that I decided to make something special. Folding my paper like a fan, and then folding it in half, it looked like it would make a fine bookmark. I colored it with flowers, and put my name in cursive on the front. Then I put a secret message in one of the folds. I wrote, "I Love God." It was my response to this event and a memento that I still possess. How true the verse is in 1 John 4:19 KJV which says, "We love Him, because He first loved us."

My parents divorced soon after that and I vividly remember the day my mom went to court. I watched as she put on a green dress suit and leaned in toward the mirror to put on a pretty pair of earrings. As I lay looking up at the seagull mobile she put above the bed so I could go to sleep at night, I asked her if Daddy would ever be coming home again. "No" she said. I lay there quietly with questions filling my head that needed answers. Was my mom not pretty enough? What could have driven our daddy away? It must be my fault, I thought, one too many kids for him to handle.

The gaping hole his absence made, the sense of security, value and direction that a father's love brings, was replaced with the gnawing sense of being rejected and abandoned, and a belief that we must not be worthwhile to stick around for.

My siblings were deeply affected, but I felt the pain of it more acutely for my three brothers. They had to borrow someone else's dad, or maybe an uncle for father/son events, which made us more aware of our loss, as though it were sending a statement to the world, how worthless we felt. For me, in all my memories the one that shaped my life the most was that I never saw my mother loved by anyone. I never saw her hugged or kissed by anyone beyond her own children. I felt so unlovable, and that I would have to be something so flawless, if I were to find someone to love me.

A five year old can hardly put in to words such an experience as I had that day, or be aware of its effect to alter ones life. But now, I can describe what it spoke to me then. God was declaring to me; "I will be your Father."

That first encounter with the Lord would be the beginning of my new Father's care over my life. It would take years before I would really know the One who had embraced me, but He placed a hunger in my heart that would eventually lead me straight to Him.

Throughout every challenge I would face, and rebellious road that I would take, I often heard the voice of my Father speaking to me; "Teri, this isn't want you want."

I thank Him for His guidance and discipline, His pity and compassion. His love has healed the little girl and has made this woman His own. And when I see the admiration and praise on the faces of earthly fathers toward their children, I can see my Father there, in my mind's eye, taking delight in me.

The Umbrella

Anna Zogg

As I hurried across five lanes of traffic, I gasped from the intolerable heat. However the mugginess concerned me less than the sky's condition. I reached my bus stop, worried by the late afternoon clouds that doubled in size and blackness.

"Please," I said in a half-prayer. "Don't let it rain." I had at least a fifteen-minute wait for my bus. Although I had brought an umbrella, I was certain it would be little protection against the threatening storm.

I sat on a bench, a short distance from a woman who perched at the very end. She threw me a hesitant smile.

"Looks like we're in for rain," I said.

She merely nodded, her gaze sidling away.

For the next several minutes, I watched—and felt—the growing storm. Across the street a trash can tipped. The contents spilled, freeing papers that twirled and danced into the air. The wind roared over cars that lined the intersection. An invisible hand shoved me, as though trying to dislodge me from the bench. A distant rumble grew louder, like a train barreling toward our location.

Beside me, a large splat of water pelted the metal bench, then another and another. I opened my umbrella, grabbing it with two hands when the wind threatened to snatch it away.

I had to raise my voice to catch the attention of the woman. "You're welcome to share this."

"Thanks. I'll be okay."

The rain continued to fall, slowly at first, then with a building tempo. Soon it beat the metal bench with hammering intensity. I pulled the umbrella more closely, staring down the street and wondering where the bus was. An endless row of cars stretched beyond sight.

"It's raining pretty hard," I said to the woman. I pointed to my umbrella.

She shook her head. Water streaked her dark hair while large droplets clung to the end of her nose.

Rain bounced off the sidewalk and bench, drenching my legs and feet. A gray curtain of water blurred the traffic just a few yards away. The papers which had danced so freely earlier now lay crushed and soaked. A torrent snatched and rushed them into the gutter.

The woman at the end of the bench hunkered over, her face hidden.

Once again I tried. "I really feel guilty hogging this umbrella to myself. You're welcome to share it."

"Oh, no," she declined a third time. "It doesn't matter at this point. Besides, my seat is dry." She indicated the bench.

By the time our bus arrived, the rain had begun to let up. But it was too late for my companion. She was soaked to the skin.

As I rode toward my destination, I shivered from the chill of the air-conditioned bus. I couldn't get the woman out of my head. Why had she refused?

I wondered if God faces the same dilemma with us. He sent Jesus to die for the sins of the world and asks, "Will you accept what My Son has done for you?"

We smile and say, "We'll be okay."

When life's struggles come our way, God offers His hand. This time we shake our heads, convinced we can solve problems ourselves.

When we're soaked and chilled by sin, we still refuse Him, declaring it's too late. Besides, we cling to that tiny dry spot—our comfort zone—rather than trust the true comfort He offers.

"Under His wings, I'll safely abide," so the song goes.

I wonder if during life's hard times, I am sometimes the woman at the end of the bench who unaccountably refuses the umbrella of God's love.

Christmas Blessing

Penelope Burbank

The large white delivery truck approached the narrow street lined with small houses.

A single address –1957—appeared on the delivery slip.

The dwelling was meager compared to the stature of the truck.

Two pairs of hands clutched the offering for a young family on Christmas Eve.

A basket of food and two thawing turkeys would relieve some of their need.

As the door opened, inviting warmth flowed out meeting the frozen night air.

Surprised faces beckoned Santa's Helpers within.

Humble voices covered the deliverers with a blanket of gratitude.

Soft drinks and warm conversation were consumed.

The young father watchful over his glowing wife great with child said, "Work will come soon."

This meek, gracious father offered a humble prayer.

Their young son sat content next to his mother, not once asking, "Will Santa come?"

His mother spoke encouragingly of her soon to be born child.

"I hope the delivery will go alright."

Two pairs of hands went to help a small family in a time of need.

Two gift-bearers left with overflowing hearts and tear-filled eyes.

The joy of Christ's love in that lowly home was greater than any worldly possession this life could offer.

Proverbs 31:10-31
New Contemporary (Per)Version

Marcia K. Hornok

King Lemuel's mother was a perceptive woman, despite her obvious hearing disability: "What, O my son? And what, O son of my womb? And what, O son of my vows?" (31:2). She taught little Lem what to look for in a woman. If this with-it mom were living today, her oracle might sound like this:

10 - Who can find a virtuous woman, for she is out jogging.

11 - The heart of her husband safely trusts in her, for they have signed a pre-nuptial agreement.

12 - She will do something good for herself every day of her life.

13 - She seeks self-fulfillment and works outside the home in a meaningful career.

14 - She is like the merchants' ships, bringing her food from take-out delis.

15 - She rises also while it is yet night, and gives lunch money to her children, and a check to their psychologist.

16 - She considers a country club and joins it. From her earnings, she buys what she wants.

17 - She girds herself with style, and improves her self image.

18 - She perceives that her tanning sessions are good. Her credit card bills go out by night.

19 - She lays out her hands to play Farmville; her thumbs text with speed.

20 - She extends her checkbook to endangered species; yes, she reaches out her hand to save the wetlands.

21 - She is not afraid of the snow for her household, for they will vacation in the Islands.

22 - She makes herself get noticed: her clothing is designer-recent.

23 - Her husband is known for his sharing of household responsibilities, and he acts unthreatened by her success.

24 - She limits her family size to 1.2 children and delivers them to the best day care centers.

25 - Her plastic surgeon shall rejoice in time to come.

26 - She opens her jewelry case with pride. In her house are many collectibles.

27 - She watches well over her favorite TV programs, and her household never eats at home together.

28 - Her children rise up and call her at the office; her

husband also, and he praises her, saying:

29 - "Many daughters have wimpy husbands, but you excel them all."

30 - Charm is phoney, and beauty is expensive; but a woman who has it all—she shall be resented.

31 - Give her the latest issue of *O* magazine, and let her be blind to what really counts beyond the Pearly Gates.

This article has been updated since it originally appeared in *Whittenburg Door*, a Christian satire magazine, in 1986. It was Hornok's first publishing credit.

The Puddin' Pond Caper

Sam Wilson

Once upon a time there was a puddin' pond filled with rich creamy chocolate. In that pond were lily pads made of white fluffy marshmallows, upon which little Hershey™ kisses lived. The pond was tucked away in a forest of candy canes and cotton candy trees.

Not many strangers came by because it was so quiet and secluded. However, one day a fellow named Crunchy Nugget, by chance while walking through the forest, came upon the pond. He was the rooten-tootenest crunchy nugget around, and he had plans to steal all the chocolate kisses. He wanted to put them into his cookies and make a special cookie treat. That sounded like it would make a fine cookie, but no matter how good it sounded it was not the right thing to do, because we know that stealing is not right.

Now the keeper of the pond went by the name "Chocolate Smoothy." When Smoothy heard that Crunchy Nugget's plan was to steal all the chocolate kisses to put them into his cookies, Smoothy had a talk with him.

Smoothy told Crunchy Nugget that he did not need to steal; that if he would have asked, Smoothy would have given him some chocolate.

Crunchy Nugget told Smoothy how sorry he was for even thinking such a thing.

So, no matter how good something looks or sounds, it is always better to ask before you take, and that's a little nugget of advice.

Grandkids

Susan Bromeland Geerdes

Scent of Fun and Family
Kringla and cookie baking aromas
tantalize, wafting through the air.
The number and kind of cookies
exponentially increase
as grandkids race one another
to see who makes the most:
over 100 tiny gingerbread men!

Explore
Adventures galore we all must do
because new ones need to know
and love our favorite spots.
This compels us on to the cabin,
the Cave, Antelope Island,
dinosaur haunts, national parks,
the Dunes, the farm, the camps,
rivers, ski slopes, fishing and more.

Listen
The thrumming beat, their music shares,
energizes, invigorates, enlivens our generation.
Talents develop; our hearts swell with pride.

Learn
Catch their first fish, bait that hook.
Swim across the pool, pass the test.

Read a book!!!! Play that game,
build a hut or tree house tall,
stand on their head, do a cartwheel,
ride a horse, pump the swing,
ride a bike, skip a rock,
row a boat, paddle the canoe,
start the motor, drive a four-wheeler.

Connect
Believe, pray and see God's help.
Make close friends that last since they were little.
They made us proud when they met their kin.
Respectful listening, sweet proximity,
warm big smiles and dazzling manners.
Helpful, useful, sense of humor and wit finely honed,
Utterly amazing in everything, good kin,

Thank you, Lord, for them.

Senior Citizen Cowboy

Sam Wilson

You know, in the morning when this old cowboy looks in the mirror, I see a lot of old creeping all over this face. Shoot, I can remember when the first smile in the mirror would bounce back an image of a full set of pearly whites. I don't even have to smile to see them now. They're sitting in that bowl of water on the countertop, looking right back at me. With a little glue I put my choppers in place for another day. Then I hobble to the shower and spend fifteen minutes under the hot water to get my motor skills back.

Now it's time to belly up to the table for a nice healthy bowl of oatmeal. Dern, I hate that stuff! Bacon and eggs goes down so much better, but I guess that wouldn't do my ticker much good. I think about feeding the cattle and horses; I might even ride old Paint up the valley. Better give her a good workout. The most exercise that horse gets anymore is chewing hay and swatting flies with her tail.

Shoot, I sure don't recall this saddle being so heavy. It's all I can do to get it on her back. She has learned a few tricks in her old age, like expanding her belly when I cinch her up. Then when I mount up she relaxes her belly—the cinch loosens up and the party's on. The saddle spins under her and I'm counting the hair on her belly. Kinda like the most thrilling amusement park ride I can stand at this age. Getting back up on her is a chore in itself. With

240 pounds and stiff knees, I dern near tip the old gal over.

I'm on my way now and doing pretty good, but fifteen minutes later I'm leading her rather than riding her. I don't remember that saddle being so uncomfortable. Why, it's got me all stoved up.

But we get up the valley, check out some cows and calves, and then start back to the ranch. That old sun is beating down, and with Paint's meandering pace I'm about to doze off when a dern jack rabbit pops up. Paint hasn't moved that fast in years. I am bouncing around like a ball on a ping pong paddle, my knees sounding like two tin cans in a gunny sack.

Soon the ranch house comes in sight. I don't know what pushed that old horse on—the fear that jack rabbit put in her or the sight of the hay stack down by the milk shed. I finally get her shut down—just in time because that low-hanging branch on the cottonwood tree up by the ditch is coming up fast. Now, I'm going to give her the benefit of the doubt. I don't think she'd want to brush me off by running under it. Would she?

Next time I'm up this way, I won't leave it to chance. I'm cutting that low branch off. She won't get a fool notion like that in her head again.

Well, I dust myself off and walk her to the shed where I unsaddle her and brush her off. Then with a couple flakes of hay, I bed her down for the night. Better feed the other livestock while I'm out here and then get my aching bones back inside the house.

A quick bite to eat and it's on to the recliner. I fall asleep so fast my eyelids slam shut. Two hours later, I'm off like a herd of turtles to walk around the house and make sure everything's okay. Then I go warm up the bed and dream of Cowboy Heaven, where there's

Grassy glades and rippling streams—that's what fills this cowboy's dreams.

Grass that stretches far as eye can see; belly deep, I'm fancy free.

A horse that's sleek and fast as the wind, cattle many and hard times slim.

This is a cowboy's heaven, at least to me.

When Christ leads me home someday, the words I hope I hear Him say are:

"Grassy glades and rippling stream, I've made for you a cowboy's dream."

"Senior Citizen Cowboy" won Second Place in the Salt Lake County Silver Pen Competition 2010.

The Real Night Before Christmas

Marcia Hornok

'Twas the night before Christmas, and all through the town
People clamor for lodging, but none can be found.
Exhausted from travel, his pregnant wife too,
Joseph searches and begs, "Any shelter will do."
At last he is offered a portion of hay
Where livestock are kept, and that's where they stay.
Poor Mary's time comes while they camp in this place.
(For the birth of a **King**, what ironic disgrace!)
She labors in silence. He shields her from view.
They are lonely and fearful, but trusting God too.
Contractions intensify. Animals stare.
They wish they were home with loved ones who care.
The stillness is pierced by a newborn's weak cry.
The miracle babe is wrapped 'till he's dry.
Tiny fingers and feet are kissed and inspected.
(One day they'll be wounded, pierced, rejected.)
He's laid in a feed trough—this **Bread of Life**.

"**Messiah** has come," Joseph says to his wife.
In glad Jewish custom, announcers are hired
when babies arrive. But this music's inspired:
"Fear not; for behold, I bring tidings of joy,
Peace, and good will through the birth of this boy."
The shepherds who hear it are first to believe.
A **Lamb** has been born, and they hurry to see.
In wonder they honor him, chuckle his chin.
Their excitement and joy causes Mary to grin.
Then we hear them exclaim (and many are awed),
"The **Savior** has come. All glory to God."
And that's the real story in rhythm and rhyme
Of the night before Christmas when **God** entered time.

Amazing Provision and Protection

Lilian P. Hosfeld

"You Filipinos are comfortable and enjoying your life here in Brunei while your countrymen are dying without Christ." Lolo (Grandfather) Victor bluntly told this during our devotion after dinner in his government housing in Brunei. This man of God volunteered as pastor of the only registered Christian fellowship center in that Muslim country.

At the age of thirty-one my life was radically changed by that message. I dedicated my life to the Lord as I decided to serve by faith. My return trip to the Philippines was paid by a friend.

I had a desire to serve in Cebu part of Visayan Island in the Philippines because that place has many people dying and claiming to be Christian but not born again. A Filipina doctor who worked in the Brunei government, my close friend and confidant, Dr. V. N. Book from Cebu, Philippines offered me a job of helping establish a plantation of spices in their big tract of land in the southern part of Cebu province. Managing the farm and ministry in the countryside did not materialize as we planned.

I knew deep in my heart that I needed to be strong in the Lord no matter what. I directly went to Cebu, Philippines from Brunei, praying and claiming God's provision and protection for me. I left all my personal belongings at the Book's residence, before I went home to see my family for goodbye and blessings. I told my parents and siblings that I had resigned from my overseas job and would do a full time volunteer mission work. My parents approved and supported my decision despite their concerns.

I did not have any support or job at that time. Two of my younger siblings were disappointed but tried to hide their feelings. One was about to enter a Medical School and another one about to start college too. They knew that my resignation means that they have to delay their plans to go to college. I told them, "Sorry, let us pray and seek the Lord's guidance. It's been a long time that God has been calling me to a full time ministry."

I lived in the Book's countryside home for a about six months while doing some buying and selling of personal care products in order to survive. I joined the worship service in a small Christian church that meets in a home. We prayed and the lay leaders told me to wait and see how God would work through the situation.

One Sunday, I decided to worship with the Metropolitan Church of Christ in the Cebu City area. I met a lady faculty member of Cebu Bible Seminary, Mrs. Dulce Labrado. She invited me for an afternoon meeting and fellowship with the Cebu Christian Ministers Association. During the meeting, the members of the Association willingly offered to work with me. They even told me to have a formal training at the Cebu Bible Seminary.

"Yes, I am willing, please pray for me." The following week, I found out that the Book family had a beach house that was close to the Seminary. They offered me to let me use it for free. What a blessing, I rejoiced in the Lord.

In the Bible Seminary they offered a free tuition as long as I maintained a certain grade. I volunteered to help with some office work and taught either the youth or children's Sunday school in one of the city congregations.

I will not forget how God delivered me from danger as I lived by myself. The beach house had a lock, one bedroom with a modest living room, and facilities for me. There was a concrete rooftop with a staircase outside where people can go up anytime. The owner had not used it for several years. People came and went on the property. The house was located in an area inhabited by poor fisherman with many alcoholics and drug addicts. My first month of living in that house was tough and discouraging. In the evening, it was hard to study and pray, and even to sleep because of the noise of the drunks and a few drug addicts. I prayed and cried to the Lord for deliverance. Some friends in the neighborhood helped me plead with the people who went up on the rooftop. We asked them to please keep quiet in the evening because the noise bothered me. They said yes, but the noise continued.

One Saturday morning, I noticed several kids and some youth were standing beside the house watching me. I could see their facial expressions showing their curiosity despite the screened window. I was terrified for a while, but just ignored the incident that day. The following Sunday, a next door neighbor told me that all the men who used to go up on the rooftop were all scared because they saw some floating white ladies (their description) around the compound. They all ran away and never bothered to go to the rooftop since then.

I praise God for that angelic visitation that makes the people believe that God always protects anyone who trusts him by faith. Even now, every time I recall that miracle I cannot express my gratitude and how I feel with words.

There was one time, as I walked by the flea market from the city congregation to the public transport station back to the Seminary that someone snatched my purse in the middle of a crowded street. I shouted and cried because that was the only money I had for my one week allowance. I told the sidewalk vendor in front of me, "Would you please help me. I am a volunteer missionary here in your area, the only money I had in that purse is from the church where I taught today." I sat crying beside the sidewalk and prayed. I declared that in Jesus' holy name that purse will be returned. It took five minutes and somebody dropped my purse in front of me. I immediately stepped on my wallet and shouted, "Praise the Lord!"

There were many mind boggling experiences of God's provision, at a time I did not know where and how the Lord would provide my need. Sometimes the church that I helped during the weekend ministry did not have money to share but our loving God provided in His own way.

One day, I went to visit a friend's home when his dad was seriously ill. They did not have the money to buy his medicine. I gave my only six hundred pesos (more or less eighteen dollars) to buy the medicine. I prayed, "God, it's up to you now to take care of me." The following day, I received mail from a family friend in Manila. They told me in the letter that few days ago after their family devotion, their four-year old son Mickey told Mom, "Let us send Lilian eight hundred pesos because she needed it badly."

I do not have any explanation to this except God marvelous provision flows to his children. I lived by faith, one day at a time for the food allowance and other expenses. The Lord always uses His faithful children as channel of blessings. I cannot recall any day that I did not have food, shoes, and clothes to wear.

From June 1990 till March 1993 was a solid three years of total dependency on God. The Lord supplied all my needs according to his glorious riches in Christ Jesus. I give all the glory and honor to God for all those blessings and for the future blessings He will bestow.

Before graduation at Cebu Bible Seminary on March 1993, they offered me a teaching position. I told them that I wanted to know and consult God for His will for me. I didn't know whether I should go back to Brunei as a missionary with a working visa like Victor or serve with them.

I went to Touch of Glory Prayer Mountain located on Mt. Buso-Buso, Antipolo City, Philippines for almost two months for forty days of prayer and full fasting including the preparation and breaking of the fast under the supervision of faithful South Korean missionaries, Paul and Esther Yo. They were the first couple to offer prayer and full fasting for the spiritual recovery of the Philippines in that prayer mountain. That opened a lot of trials and victories for me. It prepared me to be at the Cebu Bible Seminary for six years as a faculty, academic dean, and vice president including how the Lord uses me in praying and sharing the love of Jesus Christ here in Utah, USA.

Within six years of my service at the Seminary, my two sisters graduated both with Degrees in Music Ministry. Both of my sisters have happy and prosperous Christ-centered marriages while serving as volunteers in teaching and music ministry in our home church.

By September 1999, a guy from Utah visited me in Cebu Bible Seminary while I was completing my Master Degree at Cebu Normal University. We got engaged. I resigned from Cebu Bible Seminary on December 22, 1999. I came to Utah and we got married on July 8, 2000.

The Lord always opens the door of opportunity in serving him wherever He leads me. I am amazed at being God's workmanship created in Christ Jesus to pray and encourage people daily which God prepared in advance for me to do for His glory and honor. The ups and downs of my past helps me to identify to the struggling followers of Christ who has difficulty in navigating life's adversities.

Now, as I live in the United States of America, this land of abundance, there is still a broken heart in me praying for our brethren in those countries like my home country, the Philippines, where most of the faithful servants of the Lord live by faith for daily provision. They are poor physically, but richly blessed with love, hope, godly contentment, and the protection and provision by faith, as I had experienced.

Water and Light for Me

Jim Thacher

Water and light each had a prominent place during the Feast of Tabernacles because God had provided water from rocks to quench thirst and the light of the cloud by day and the fire by night to guide Israel during its wilderness wanderings (Exodus 17:6 and 13:21).

The Jews celebrated this feast during Jesus' lifetime on earth (John 7:2). Each morning during the feast a delegation went to the Pool of Siloam to fill a golden pitcher and pour it on the temple altar, to symbolically flow down into the city and the surrounding area. "In the last day, that great day of the feast, Jesus stood and cried, saying, If any man thirst, let him come unto me, and drink. He that believeth on me, as the scripture hath said, out of his belly shall flow rivers of living water" (John 7:37-38).

Concerning light, the priests' garments from the previous year were fashioned into wicks for the fire in four candelabras in the women's court of the temple. The light could be seen all over the city of Jerusalem. Against this background Jesus made the statement, "I am the light of the world: he that followeth me shall not walk in darkness, but shall have the light of life" (John 8:12).

The next chapter of John's gospel describes the healing of a blind man. Jesus repeats to him the words "I am the light of the world" (John 9:5b). The blind man gains his physical sight and exclaims, "One thing I know, that, whereas I was blind, now I see"

(John 9:25b). This healing followed the obedience of the man born blind to wash in the pool of Siloam, the same body of water from which the priests drew the water to pour on the altar at the top of the temple mount.

But Jesus did not stop at physical healing. He sought out the man and assured his spiritual healing as well. In John 9:35b-38 the narrative continues. "Dost thou believe on the Son of God? He answered and said, Who is he, Lord, that I might believe on him? And Jesus said unto him, Thou hast both seen him, and it is he that talketh with thee. And he said, Lord, I believe. And he worshipped him."

So too we may come to Jesus and drink of that life-giving stream in the desert of man's ideas. The word picture Christ draws for us is that of a river flowing from the mount of God that satisfies our thirst. We need only believe or trust in Him for the water symbolizing our salvation.

As we continue in our relationship with Christ, we walk in the light of His presence. Then we avoid the obstacles obscured by darkness and are guided by God's light. Like the man born blind in John's gospel we may exclaim, "One thing I know, that, whereas I was blind, now I see" (John 9:25b).

The Barren Fig Tree

Teresa Hanly

Matthew 21:19-20

The tree stands alone by the roadside, amid the arid backdrop of the city. By the look of it, the bark and the shape of the leaves, one can detect which kind of fruit it would bear. This one is a fig tree. It bears fruit three different times of the year: June, August and December. Sometimes the latter figs hang on the tree until spring. This tree is unusual however, as it produced leaves early, but no fruit.

The symbolic message found in the passage of the Bible in Matthew that I find most applicable for us today is that of the sinister nature of being fooled by appearances. That outwardly, a person may portray characteristics and attributes that might classify them as Christians, but when the Lord approaches the tree to partake of its fruit, there is none. And He curses that tree.

Jesus says in Matthew 7:13-20 "Enter ye in at the strait gate: for wide is the gate, and broad is the way, that leadeth to destruction, and many there be which go in thereat: Because strait is the gate, and narrow is the way, which leadeth unto life, and few there be that find it. Beware of false prophets, which come to you in sheep's clothing, but inwardly they are ravening wolves. Ye shall know them by their fruits. Do men gather grapes of thorns, or figs of thistles? Even so, every good tree bringeth forth good fruit, but a corrupt tree bringeth forth evil fruit. A good tree cannot bring forth evil fruit, neither can a corrupt tree bring forth good fruit. Every tree that bringeth not forth good fruit is hewn down, and cast into the fire. Wherefore, by their fruits ye shall know them.

We find ourselves in a world where it acceptable for us to customize a faith and doctrine that suits our personal preferences, a watered down assortment of "truths" causing us to stray from *The Truth* in small measures, bit by bit.

If outward conformity to the principles of religion is above addressing the need for a confession of faith in Christ or the challenge to be His follower in manner of life, we make it hard to detect those who genuinely profess Christ as Lord, and so, we are challenged to inspect fruit. A gradual and subtle deception that will claim the lives of many, the harder it becomes to distinguish Christians from the rest of the world.

It is good for us to answer some tough questions to ourselves if we are not to be found wanting on the day of His return.

What arguments do we make when taking our positions?

What justifications are hanging upon our branches?

At what price did we buy the illusion of our false security?

When the Lord approaches us, what fruit does He find there?

Do we believe?

Psalm 1

Blessed is the man that walketh not in the counsel of the ungodly, nor standeth in the way of sinners, nor sitteth in the seat of the scornful. But his delight is in the law of the LORD; and in his law doth he meditate day and night. And he shall be like a tree planted by the rivers of water, that bringeth forth his fruit in his season; his leaf also shall not wither; and whatsoever he doeth shall prosper. The ungodly are not so: but are like the chaff which the wind driveth away. Therefore the ungodly shall not stand in the judgment, nor sinners in the congregation of the righteous. For the LORD knoweth the way of the righteous: but the way of the ungodly shall perish.

The First Christmas Tree
A Parable—Almost

Jim Cook

The wind blew softly in the meadow just below the timberline. The clouds had lifted and the sheep were shadowy white puffs of wool in the moonlight.

The chill of a late spring[1] still hung in the air. The shepherds, having gathered the sheep into semi-repose in their pen, were finishing the last of their dinner and lounging comfortably by the remains of the cookfire.

The land they sat upon was ancient. Here the long-gone Canaanites had built their altars to pagan gods and goddesses in a natural hollow. The rocks had watched silently with their predecessors two thousand years before as Abraham[2] gathered wood for sacrifice with young Isaac by his side. They had heard the ram bleating in the thicket as Isaac was redeemed.

It was here that David had killed a bear that attacked his sheep, while he was still a boy.[3] Here had fled David when pursued by Saul. And here he had sheltered his company of men before becoming king, spreading their

---

[1]Although the birth of Christ is traditionally celebrated in December, it is to be remembered that there were shepherds in the field with their sheep at the time. Many believe that a late spring or early summer time period would be more accurate.

[2]Genesis 22:1-14. The reference to the region of Moriah in verse 2 is frequently interpreted to refer to an area near where Jerusalem was later built.

[3]1 Samuel 17:34-35

rations on the same flat boulder at the edge of the grove, drinking from the same brook, and singing and telling tall stories as they warmed themselves before the fire. Sometimes the air had been clear, as tonight. Sometimes wind and rain and storm had bellowed in the sky.

Others had been there, too, over the years. Bandits and robbers. Soldiers and hunters. Picnickers and lovers. And animals too numerous to count—rabbits and coneys and bears.

The brook and the trees and the rocks had seen it all. Over the years the stream had grown deeper, the trees taller and straighter. And the stones had observed it all, unmoved.

One young sapling tree, straighter and taller than those around, quivered silently and watched. It "thought" about similar nights in the past, and perhaps about the future.

Of course, the tree could not remember all the long centuries. It was not old enough. But the rocks—who had been there—had recounted their tales, and the tree held no doubts.

High-flying remnants of the earlier clouds skittered past the treetops silver-laced by the moon's light. The sky darkened as it cleared and the brilliant beauty of the Milky Way stood out like lamplight against the black mantle.

The shepherds thought about their stomachs and talked about the need to meet the new head tax with the required Roman coin that bore the picture of the man who claimed to be God.[4] And they complained about the census, the second that the Caesar had dared to impose in barely two years.[5]

---

[4]Caesar had placed his likeness on the most common coinage, declared himself to be God, and required that he be worshiped by payment of taxes with that coin. Jewish coinage was not acceptable.

[5]Roman records show that there had been a census and taxation only two years before.

Perhaps it was the tree who saw first the change in the night sky.

The change was subtle as it began, a shifting of the light as though a cloud passed from in front of the moon, casting a brighter ray upon the meadow and bathing it in a brilliant glow.

The stars seemed to become sharper, and then suddenly closer as though the galaxy were in motion. But no! More of them shone now. More stars, more lights in the sky, and the new ones seemed to draw closer to the earth and to the little cluster of men and sheep nestled in the grove and the meadow, their brilliance making the others seem pale by comparison. The tree watched in wonder as all that it knew of nature seemed to change.

The shepherds began to point and shout as the sparkling points of light swirled against the darkness of the night, and then they stood transfixed with terror as the beautiful display swooped and dipped toward them in a myriad of shining colors.

Only the sheep were undisturbed. And the rocks. And the brook. And the trees.

The tall tree marveled and trembled with excitement, its branches twitching imperceptibly as it watched.

And suddenly, the scene changed yet again. One of the lights, a glowing orb, left the others and came to rest, ever so lightly, beside the fire so that its embers seemed dim now by contrast. And instead of the orb, the figure of a man stood before them.

For a moment the tree was confused, and then it understood, if the men did not at first. This was an angel, and the light was the glory of the Creator shining around them.

The shepherds were overwhelmed with fear. But the angel spoke with a gentle voice that was soothing and comforting and warm. And as he spoke their terror dropped like a cloak beside the bed at the end of the day.

"Don't be afraid! I bring you good news of great joy for everyone."[6]

Something in his voice captured their thoughts and transformed them with eager attention, no longer frightened.

"Today," he said in a voice that beamed with pleasure at the telling, "in the city of David a Savior has been born to you—Christ the Lord."

One of the shepherds, braver than the rest, or perhaps more foolish and disturbed, answered back. "Many have claimed to be the Promised One. How will we know which is real?"

The tree moved its upper branches, as though to nod. It had heard many people—both men and women—talk of the Messiah during its lifespan. The Deliverer who would rescue them from Roman bondage. The King who would sit upon the throne of David. The Prince of Peace. Some had spoken in hope. Some in despair. Some in jest.

The angel spoke quietly. "This will be a sign for you: You will find the baby wrapped in strips of cloth and lying in a manger."

For a moment the bold shepherd seemed as though he might dare to venture another question. But the angel gave no opportunity for speech, his message clearly given.

One moment he stood among them. The next he was above them, and suddenly the entire host of sparkling lights resolved itself into thousands upon thousands of angels, and the one who had spoken was lost among them.

And then came a sound, such as never had been heard before in the little hollow, and the grove, and the meadow. It was soft at first, like the wind, and then it swelled and rose until even a roaring waterfall would have been lost in its embrace.

---

[6]Luke 2:10*ff*

The noise of stringed instruments, and percussion, and trumpets all blended together in one harmonious melody, beyond anything imagined before on the earth. Majesty and beauty and sweetness enthralled men and nature alike as the sound of Heaven rang across the hills.

And then the angels began to sing, as they must have sung in chorus at the Creation,[7] as they must sing around the holy throne[8] of the Creator. The words were simple, repeated over and over again until they reached crescendoing climax:

"Glory to God in the highest!
And on earth, peace to the people
with whom he is pleased."

And then they were gone.

Without warning. There was no slow retreat as there had been an entrance. Music swelled one moment, silence the next.

As the men began to recover and to speak, the tall tree listened and pondered. It had seen and heard a miracle. Something that went beyond all that the rocks had told from the past. Something that spoke of the future—and the present.

Beneath its branches, the shepherds talked of what they had seen. Some wondered what it meant and why. Some wondered what to do.

The bold shepherd had the answer. "Let's go to the city of David and see." A murmur rippled through the group and a nod. "Yes. Let us see this mighty thing the Lord has told us about."

And they left. All of them. So excited were they that they left the sheep, and all of their belongings, and they went to Bethlehem where David had been born so long ago. And the trees and the rocks and the brook, and

[7]Job 38:4-7
[8]Revelation 5:11-14

especially the tall tree, stood silent vigil, awaiting their return.

High above, the clouds again skittered past as moonlight dripped through the branches of the trees, mottling the ground with silver, and the Milky Way shone quietly with a fiery glow.

And when the new day came, silence blanketed the meadow except for the bleating of sheep. No predator came to steal a meal from the flock. No thief wandered by to claim the goods left unattended.

The day dragged slowly by and then, as at last twilight began to lengthen its shadows and the sun began to turn the scattered clouds first to gold, then to red, and at last to gray, the tree heard voices in the distance.

The silence was transformed by the music of laughter and jest, and even singing, though none of the shepherds had a good voice. They were joyful, and as they sang the tree heard remembered words from the Psalms, some of which young David had composed in this very grove.

The shepherds had found a baby wrapped in cloth strips in an emptied feeding trough in the company of Mary and Joseph, just as the angel had said. They were overcome. They knew that this was the One! It was all true!

Sunlight faded away into darkness as the shepherds, having seen to their flock, sank in comfort before the fire. They talked of the amazement of the people they had told about the child, and about the angels.

Some had thought them drunk. But they knew better. They had seen exactly what they had been told they would see. And could an angel tell less than the truth?

They gazed eagerly at the stars so far away in the glistening sky and hoped for another visitation. And they left off their usual complaining and praised the Creator and gave Him glory for all they had seen and heard.

And above them, its leaves sheltering them from the night, the first Christmas tree pondered deeply and wondered what might transpire next.

Many years came and went in this little grove. Seasons blended into seasons. Shepherds and flocks came and went, as did soldiers and hunters and picnickers and lovers and travelers. The meadow and the brook and the stones remained unchanged. The trees grew taller, and occasionally one fell from age or storm, becoming the next source of fuel for fire. Occasionally, a tree was cut deliberately, but not often.

Although it was now straight and strong and no longer a sapling, the tall tree was somehow left alone to grow and expand its branches and think its thoughts.

Every time the meadow and the grove were occupied and people rested beneath the trees or ate on the flat boulder or warmed themselves by the fire pit, the tree listened hopefully and remembered that night long ago when it had witnessed the announcement to the shepherds. It listened especially well when those same men returned with their flock, as most of them did during the first few years.

Sometimes they talked about that night, lounging comfortably by the fire in the evening with their sheep gently settled. Mostly they complained about the growing Roman abuses. They thought about their stomachs as usual, and about their homes, and about their amusements, and about the latest news and gossip.

At first they talked eagerly about the baby in the manger and hoped for the future. And the tree listened and dreamed along with them as they talked about the day when the baby would grow up to be the King of the Jews, and the man on the Roman throne who pretended to be God would be gone, along with the imposter king Herod who sat on the throne in Jerusalem.

And always, they watched the stars that never changed, sparkling in the darkness as they had done night after night for centuries.

One night, only a few months, perhaps a year, after that first magical night, it had been different, and the shepherds had roused in excitement. No clouds obscured the sky that night. A gentle zephyr breeze had moved even the faintest wisps from view. And in the eastern sky was something new, a star that even the ancient rocks could not remember, a brilliant jewel shining brighter than any other sparkle in the sky.

The tree watched in wonder for another visit from the angels, as excited in its way as the shepherds, listening for the first notes of that spell-binding symphony that had come with the first announcement.

But although they watched for the entire night, the men barely remembering to keep the fire glowing, nothing happened, and the dawn greeted them with a glorious display of pink and silver that somehow they didn't see.

The star returned that night and the next night and so on for many nights, seeming each night to appear closer than it had been the night before. The first few nights the shepherds watched eagerly, still filled with excitement, still hoping for another visit from the sparkling lights.

But as time went on they lost interest in the nightly miracle, thinking of it as ordinary, as people do when miracles come every day, until at last only the trees and the rocks and the brook kept watch in wonder.

Sometimes it rained, or the new star was hidden behind the veil of spreading clouds, but always the tree managed to catch a glimpse as the new light grew so close it seemed to be almost overhead.

And then it was gone.

Without warning. The star shone brightly one night, and the next it was gone.

The shepherds, having fed their flock until the grass in the meadow had been reduced to stubble, had already moved on to greener pastures. The tree had no person to offer comment about the missing star.

And then one night the grove was filled again with men. Tired men, grimy and sweaty, tying their horses to the trees and talking and joking coarsely. Soldiers. Polishing their swords and talking about murder.

The tree listened in horror as they talked about the atrocity they had performed at king Herod's command that day in Bethlehem. Killing children! Every child under two years old. Even the soldiers, used to making excuses, seemed to think it strange to kill the children when they were not at war.

And then, the soldiers, too, were gone with dayrise and the grove was empty of travelers for many days until two of the original shepherds returned to stop at the flat boulder for a midday meal.

"It is no use, Jonas!" said one. "The king has had all of the children killed. He could not abide the thought that the Promised One would be King, and now he has killed him."

The bold shepherd, whose name was Jonas, shook his head. "He was the Christ!"

"He is dead."

Jonas spoke impetuously. "There is no reason to go on hoping, then. I will not come here again. I have been thinking long, and I have decided to stop tending sheep and start a business for myself as I should have done before."

"What will you do?"

"I will buy a boat."

"How can you pay for such a thing. Your wage is too small."

"My mother-in-law will house us for a while. I will see to it that my son, Simon, will grow to be a successful fisherman, not a feeder of sheep."

The tree lost interest in the conversation and thought about what it had heard, about the angel's promise, about the Heavenly choir, about the baby child, and about the murders, and it wondered how it could be.

After that first year, all went back to being routine. The years passed quickly and the tree no longer heard mention of the child or the angels. The shepherds changed one by one until all of the faces in the grove were new, and none remembered that glorious night save the trees and the rocks and the brook.

Then one day after many years had gone by two men came leading a donkey cart, one man much older than the other so that they seemed to be father and son.

They had come seeking wood. At first, as they began to cut among the timber that had already fallen, choosing carefully only the wood that was lengthy and intact, the tree thought that they were scavengers, just as scavengers had come in the past. And then, as they worked, it knew differently.

These were carpenters. Ruthless professionals who soon would begin to carve the grove to stumps to obtain lumber for buildings and furniture. The flat rock, the oldest of the stones, confirmed that it had happened occasionally over the years. Sometimes it took decades for the mangled grove to recover.

The tree didn't understand fear, but it knew unease as the first of its companions fell to the ground. Conversation passed between the two men and made it clear that they had not come to take all the wood, only enough to fill the cart so that they could build a special piece of furniture for a wealthy customer. And so they wanted only the strongest timber and the best.

It was the older man who first pointed at the tree.

"We'll take this one next."

The younger man, perhaps twenty-five or so, shook his head and drew near the tree.

"Let's take another, father. This one is too good to waste for such a purpose. It will have an even better use some day."

And at that instant the tree experienced the most exciting event of its lifespan, as the young carpenter reached out and touched the rough bark of its trunk. There was a brief moment for which there can be no description.

And then the tree shivered with untold pleasure as the Creator touched His Creation.

The rocks and the trees and the meadow knew immediately what had happened, and the brook began to sing as it had never sung in all its centuries. The Promised One had lived! Had they the means, the trees would at that moment have clapped their hands and the whole hillside would have shouted out with joy.[9]

And then the two were gone.

Night and day came again and one day blended into the next, season into season. Shepherds and travelers and other visitors came and went and the tree reflected often on the words of the young carpenter.

Finally, as the years passed, the tree heard an occasional reference to a prophet who had suddenly appeared. Some debated where he came from and who he was. Some said that he was just a carpenter. And the tree listened with wonder and waited and listened some more.

Then disaster struck without warning.

It was a cool day in the early spring. Snow still stood on the Judean hillsides, and angry clouds stood threatening in the sky.

---

[9]Isaiah 55:12. "For ye shall go out with joy, and be led forth with peace: the mountains and the hills shall break forth before you into singing, and all the trees of the field shall clap *their* hands."

Rough men came with teams of horses and began cruelly cutting down the grove with brutal blows of axes and saws. Loggers! With no restraint. Men for hire contracted to the Roman overlords, wantonly destroying what had stood for a thousand years.

They showed no mercy. Every tree in the grove fell to their blows as cold iron bit remorselessly into living timber. On the hard ground they stripped the branches and leaves away leaving the once proud sentinels as nothing more than naked logs. The beautiful spring foliage became withering debris beneath the woodsmen's feet.

They showed no compassion and no clemency. Fortunately, the tree felt no pain, only strange sensations and disorientation as it came under attack and then fell heavily to an unfamiliar position, prone on the ground beside its fellows. Helplessness overwhelmed it momentarily as the men removed its limbs so that they never again would wave gracefully in the gentle breeze, their leaves making music as they rustled.

In almost four decades of life the tree had grown very tall even though it was slim for its height. So tall that it would not fit intact onto the lumber wagon. And so more strange sensations raced through the trunk as the men severed it into three separate lengths to make it ready for transport.

In spite of its trauma, the tree did not lose its consciousness. Instead, its awareness seemed to sharpen, its unease growing as the oxcart carried it away from the only home it had known. Away from the rocks. Away from the brook. Away from the pasture.

The journey seemed long, though it took only a few hours. But the bumping and jostling and jerking of the cart had the effect of stretching time like a rope about to break. Until at last they came to a city. A place of noise and chaos.

And people. So many people. The tree heard their voices all around over the creaking of the cart and the clopping of the oxen hooves.

It had heard people talk of cities in the grove, but this was different than expected. The sheer size of it was beyond imagination, and the row of buildings and silent trees rising high above the sides of the cart seemed endless as they moved ahead pace by pace.

Then they were there—wherever "there" might be. The place was dark and unpleasant, surrounded by walls. The cart finally stopped and the timber was thrown down to lie inert on the cold earth, unable to see more than a patch of the sky.

And the tree wondered—why? Why was its life and its sap draining away so strangely as this in so terrible a place? And it reflected on the unfulfilled hopes it had had for the future and the promise of the carpenter.

Beyond the walls strange and intriguing sounds penetrated from the street and occasional shouts exploded as though some great event were taking place. And the tree lay in its places and continued to ponder as the light beyond the walls faded into the darkness of night.

Morning came at last, and with it more men, Roman soldiers this time, serious and loud.

"Those three."

One of the soldiers pointed at the pieces of the tree, and once again it was loaded into a cart, smaller this time, and drawn through the city streets, bumping and bouncing.

The trip was short. The cart rolled to a stop next to a high wall surrounding a building so large it towered above the wall and the trees within, its facades gleaming in the early light. A palace. The home of a king.

And the tree wondered with hope if this were the home of the Promised One. Was this the palace of the King of the Jews?

But its hopes were shattered.

A noise broke the early morning stillness, and suddenly more soldiers thrust a man roughly through an open gate toward the cart, laughing and jeering and mocking: "Hail, 'King' of the Jews!"[10]

A rough crown of inch-long locust thorns had been jammed into his head, and crimson blood flowed freely down his face and into his beard and his hair, mixing with more blood that seeped from beneath his robe.

The soldiers shoved the man to the end of the cart and forced him to drag the largest and heaviest length of the tree off the bed and carry it upon his back, so that he staggered beneath its weight and shuddered in pain as the rough bark dug into his already-damaged flesh. And as he did so the blood of the Promised One mingled with the sap of the dying tree.

With amazement the tree recognized once again the touch of its Creator. This was the Promised One. The King. The Prince of Peace. And the tree remembered the words spoken at its side so many years ago by the young carpenter: "This one will have an even better use."

The victim and his persecutors began a procession through the streets, the soldiers and many in the gathering crowd making fun and ridiculing the man who was barely able to carry the weight of the tree. Others in the crowd were weeping and mourning.

At last the soldiers tired of their sport and became impatient with the slow progress. In an instant they seized a large black man[11] from the crowd and placed the tree upon his strong back, forcing him to carry it.

---

[10]Matthew 27:29

[11]Simon the Cyrenean (Matthew 27:32) was from Cyrene, a Greek city in northern Africa. By tradition, it is believed that although he was Jewish, he was also black. His selection to carry the cross suggests that he was large and strong in appearance.

They passed through the city gate and along the highway until they came to a prominent hill near the road. "Golgotha," said someone in the crowd. The Place of the Skull. The place of execution.

The weary man was made to climb the steep hillside, the ruthless soldiers giving him no time to rest.

At a level place near the top, facing the road, they stopped at last, forcing the man to the ground, along with two other prisoners who had been in the procession.

The length of tree was laid on the ground next to the broken body of the man, and the other two lengths, which had been brought in the cart, were thrown alongside.

The man was offered a drink filled with drugs, but he refused. And the soldiers stripped off all his clothes and laid him on top of the tree, his hands raised high above his head.[12]

And then the incredible happened. The tree raged in disbelief as a soldier used a heavy mallet to drive an iron spike through the man's hands and deep into the heart of the tree. And another drove a second spike through his crossed feet as he writhed in agony.

And the tree was placed upright in a deep hole in the ground as the Promised One, the Deliverer, hung in bitter distress, beginning already to suffocate as the muscles of his chest tightened against the pain and gravity, restricting his breathing.

And as the tree tried to understand how the Creator could allow His creatures to torture and torment Him so, He spoke. Not to the crowd. But to another who was also present but unseen.

"Father, forgive them because they do not know what they are doing."[13]

---

[12]Although traditional pictures depict the cross as two pieces of wood, a pole and a crosspiece, it is probable that in a land where wood was scarce, the soldiers would have used the more traditional Roman gibbet, or single pole, instead.

[13]Luke 23:34

And the Son of God was crucified at nine o'clock in the morning with a sign nailed above His head that said:

THIS IS
JESUS OF NAZARETH
THE KING OF THE JEWS

And as He hung suffering the soldiers divided up His clothes as booty for themselves, while the religious people in the crowd made fun of Him.

Even one of the other prisoners, who was in agony himself, joined in the scorn. "Aren't you the Messiah? Then save yourself and us."

But the other prisoner rebuked him for it. And then he said: "Jesus, remember me when you come into your kingdom."

And Jesus answered. "I tell you the truth. Today you will be with me in Paradise."[14]

And the tree marveled at His compassion and understood and felt renewed and invigorated at the reassuring touch of the Creator.

This was why He was here, His lifeblood soaking into the wood and spilling upon the ground. This was what He came for, the little baby the angels had announced, the Prince of Peace, the Messiah. He came for this moment. He was born to die. So that others could be forgiven and live. The wonder of it all was too much for the tree.

He had not come as King—although the tree sensed in confusion that that would come later, after He had died. He came as Savior and Redeemer instead, paying an immeasurable price to save others instead of Himself.

And the tree was privileged to be a part of it.

After about three hours of voiceless pain Jesus turned His head toward a woman in the crowd, and instantly the tree knew that she was His mother. And His compassion

---

[14]Luke 23:43

included care that she was growing old and that He would be gone.

And He said to her: "Woman, here is your son," and to the man standing next to her: "Here is your mother."[15]

Then, having taken care of the needs of others, He rested. And the tree felt His agony as His weight tore His flesh and his bones were pulled from their sockets and His breathing became an almost impossible effort.

As the sun rose in the noon sky, at the brightest part of the day, there was a sudden blackness that obscured the sun and covered the land. It was a fearful time for a world of men that presumed to reject their Creator and Savior.

For three long hours the darkness continued as the tree reflected on the shame and suffering and humiliation being poured out before spectators on the Promised One who had come to redeem them. Foolish! It thought. Unbelievably foolish and evil and selfish. Incredible.

And then His real agony, more than the physical, was suddenly obvious as Jesus cried out in a loud voice: "*Eloi, Eloi, lama sabachthani?*" (My God, My God, why have you forsaken me?")[16] And the only sinless person who ever lived carried on Himself the sin of every other.[17]

And the tree shuddered. How much more could there be?

But even as the tree reeled in horror, it knew that Jesus had done what He had come to do. And it listened as He said, "I am thirsty."[18] And a man soaked a sponge in vinegar[19] and held it to His lips.

When He finished drinking, Jesus spoke in triumph: "It is finished."[20]

---

[15]John 19:26-27

[16]Matthew 27:46; Psalm 22

[17]Isaiah 53:1-6

[18]John 19:28

[19]Literally, "Sour wine." This was laced with myrhh, a pain-inhibiting narcotic. *cf* Matthew 27:34.

[20]John 19:30

Then He bowed His head and said, "Father, into your hands I commend my spirit."[21]

And it was done. The most awful deed of history reached its climax. And the most wonderful.

God, in human flesh, died that day. Voluntarily.

And at that moment a great earthquake boiled under the darkened sky and the tree watched in awe as the very rocks broke into pieces. In the great temple in the city, the foot-thick curtain that separated the people from the holiest place of all was torn from top to bottom. And graves came open in the earthquake, and many dead people were returned to life.

The soldiers came then, and they put a sword through His side and into His heart, but there was no need because He was already dead.

Then others came, and took His body down from the tree and carried Him away to a place in a nearby garden. From its vantage on the hill the tree could see as they buried the Redeemer in a cave and rolled a stone weighing many tons across the entrance.

And the tree reflected on the irony of it all and remembered the shepherds talking about the faraway Roman emperor and about the false king who sat upon the throne in Jerusalem. And it thought about the man who had died, the Promised One, the real King, and how different they were.

One was a man who claimed to have become God. One was a simple imposter. And the other was the one and only God who had chosen to become a man.

> "He came unto His own, and His own received Him not. But to as many as received Him, to them gave He the authority to become the sons of God, even to them that believe on His name."[22]

---

[21]Luke 23:46

Three days later, the tree received a final surprise. It was early dawn on a beautiful morning. Birds were singing and flowers bloomed on the hillside and in the garden below.

The tree was weak now, the last of its sap almost gone. Suddenly, another earthquake broke the calm, and the huge stone trembled for a moment and then, as though moved by invisible hands, rolled away from the entrance to the cave.

And there, the dying tree saw with astonishment and growing excitement, Jesus stood in the opening and walked in the garden.

And then the tree knew without a doubt that the Promised One had proven that He was able to keep His own promises. He had triumphed over death and now the Living One promised Life for the dying.

And the first Christmas tree spoke silently to its Creator: "Thank you, Lord."

THE BEGINNING

---

[22]John 1:11-12

About the Authors

Peggy Bert is a graduate of Upper CLASS Speakers, a Certified *Personality Plus* Trainer, a private pilot and holds an M. A. in Theological Studies. A popular speaker for conferences and retreats, her topics specialize in personal growth, communication skills and relationships. Publishing credits include Chicken Soup and *Marriage Partnership Magazine*.

Penelope Burbank is a teacher at a Utah middle school. Eighteen years of teaching has taught her that everyone has a story. She believes that healing comes from sharing your story with others. Hearing stories, especially from her grandchildren, enlightens and encourages her.

Mildred Irene Lee accepted the Lord as her Savior at a one-room school house which served as a church on weekends. She married **Russell Norman Champlin** in 1955, and two years later they moved with their three month old son to serve as missionaries in Brazil where they have been active in Christian Literature work for the past forty years.

Jim Cook attended the Moody Bible Institute of Chicago, retired from Utah State Government and is an active member of Utah Christian Writers Fellowship. He writes in several genres. His first novel, *The Third Hand*, an adventure/mystery for young adults, is due for publication in early 2012. Email him at jim@cyber-servant.com

Colby Russell Drane: My name is Colby Drane. I was born in Forest, Louisiana and accepted Christ as my personal savior from an early age. I fully gave my life to

Christ March 14th, 2010. I currently live in Utah, writing fiction and praising God.

Mark Francis and his wife Laura live in Sandy, Utah, with their four children. He enjoys spending time with his family, the outdoors, cooking, writing and encouraging his family and friends with God's heart for them.

Susan Bromeland Geerdes, a retired English and special education teacher, lives in Utah with her husband Ron. With a B.S. from Minnesota State University and M.Ed. from the University of Utah, she also earned numerous awards during a very blessed 25 year career helping people with disabilities gain employment.

Teresa Hanly: I've been married 34 years, and have six grown sons and two grandchildren. I minister and teach God's word to women in prison. Over the years, I have enjoyed writing life experiences and lessons that reflect God nature and acts of love He still performs today.

Marcia Hornok, managing editor of *CHERA* magazine, raised her six children in Salt Lake City where her husband pastors Midvalley Bible Church. She loves interacting with grandkids, partnering with her husband in ministry, and playing Spider Solitaire. Her credits include articles in seven devotional books, 60 different periodicals, six children's curriculum books, two mini-inspiration books, and a "Biblical Truths" column in Examiner.com.

Lilian P. Hosfeld has been an Intercessor since 1987. She considers Amy Barkman as her spiritual mentor and intercession has done more than she ever dreamed. She loves to prayer walk with her hubby's walking buddies for her: Ruby (Rottweiler), Toby (Chihuahua), and Xander (Mini Doberman Pinscher).

Consultant **L.T. Kodzo,** author of *Locker 572,* is contracted to support business operations for the Department of Defense at the Pentagon. As a dynamic speaker and sought-after facilitator, people identify with her ability to dissect complicated ideas into digestible slices. Her tumultuous youth has drawn her to champion the edgy issues young people face.

Josiah Marshall was born and raised in southern Utah and became an avid lover of the outdoors. He spent several years traveling and working in National Parks. He is currently enrolled at Moody Bible Institute to become a Christian counselor. He currently resides with his wife, Heather, in Murray, Utah.

Kim Malkogainnis: I have been writing for about 25 years. Besides writing, God allowed me to work as an extra on the TV series, "Touched By An Angel." My favorite Bible verse is I John 4:10: "Here is love: not that we loved God, but that He loved us, and sent His Son to be the atoning sacrifice for our sins."

Angela Rednour is a native Utahn who loves to write. She is a Freelance writer for Examiner.com, a play writer for her church and she also writes a blog about her journey through life, with God. Besides writing, she loves spending time crocheting, reading and playing with her cats and ferrets.

Mary Jo Sanger has been writing all her life. As a handicapped child she had to entertain herself and wrote on every paper she could find. She has written and taught Bible studies for 40 years and is currently working on her first novel. Married to Roger for 32 years, they have seven children, 14 grand children, and 5 great grandchildren so far.

Julie "JOY!" Turvey Scott has penned several personal histories, over twenty songs, and has the gift of delivering virtual hugs via cards and email. She has served as president of the Utah Christian Writers Fellowship since 2005.

Pam Sherburne has worked for a school district for twenty-eight years. She has written a number of articles and is currently a reporter for a local newspaper. She and her husband of forty-one years, have three adult children and twelve grandchildren. She enjoys spending time with her family, reading, writing and doing crafts.

Virginia Smith has published twenty Christian novels and over fifty articles. Ginny writes a variety of styles, from lighthearted relationship stories to breath-snatching suspense. Her books have been finalists for the Carol Award, Daphne du Maurier Award, and Maggie Award. *A Daughter's Legacy* received a 2011 Holt Medallion Award of Merit. www.VirginiaSmith.org

Jim Thacher is a retired rocket scientist. Publications include articles in technical journals, *The Christian Communicator*, *The Toastmaster Magazine*, anthologies of poetry and Rescue Mission Bible studies. He and his wife of 52 years work in the Awana youth club. Jim tutors junior-high math. He has 3 sons and 11 grandchildren.

Rose Turnbow: I have been married 34 years to my loving husband, Kip. We live in the beautiful Salt Lake Valley with Molly, our border collie. My life's pleasures are playing with my grandkids or kayaking, and I enjoy writing for children and sharing stories of my family's past.

Sam Wilson was born and raised on a ranch in Green River, Utah, and farmed it himself for ten years. Since 1984 he's written personal experience, humor, inspirational poetry, and children's stories. He lives in Taylorsville, Utah with his wife and teenage son but heads to the old homestead in Green River every chance he gets.

Anna Zogg: After a grade school friend introduced her to the art of writing, Anna was hooked. She has dabbled in anecdotes, short stories and devotionals, but her love is speculative fiction. Although she is a world traveler, Anna considers Utah her home.

About Utah Christian Writers Fellowship

What We Believe

Bible
We believe the Bible to be the inspired, the only infallible, authoritative Word
of God.

God
We believe in the Trinity, one Triune God, eternally existent in three Persons:
Father, Son and Holy Spirit.

Jesus Christ
We believe in the deity of our Lord Jesus Christ, in His virgin birth, in His sinless life, in His miracles, in His vicarious and atoning death through His shed blood, in His bodily resurrection, in His ascension to the right hand of the Father, and in His personal return in power and glory.

Salvation
We believe that salvation of the lost and sinful is a gift of God's grace through a person's faith in the Lord Jesus Christ.

Holy Spirit
We believe in the present ministry of the Holy Spirit by Whose Indwelling the Christian is enabled to live a godly life.

Resurrection
We believe in the resurrection of both the saved and the lost; they that are saved unto the resurrection of life and they that are lost unto the resurrection of damnation.

Believers
We believe in the spiritual unity of believers in our Lord Jesus Christ.

Utah Christian Writers Fellowship, a chapter of American Christian Writers, meets monthly in the Salt Lake City area. All Christian writers are welcome. For more information, visit www.UtahChristianWriters.com, or write to the publisher of this book at: Next Step Books, P.O. Box 70271, West Valley City, UT 84170.

14540971R00087

Made in the USA
Lexington, KY
05 April 2012